What's Your Problem?

Discovering God's Greatness in the Midst of Your Storms

EMILY A. EDWARDS, PH.D.

Living Hope Publishing ▪ Midland, Texas

LIVING HOPE PUBLISHING
P.O. Box 2153
Midland, TX 79702
www.LivingHopePublishing.com

Book design by TLC Graphics, *www.TLCGraphics.com*
Cover: Tamara Dever

Scripture quotations are from The ESV ® Bible (The Holy Bible, English Standard Version ®), copyright © 2001 by Crossway, a publishing ministry of Good News Publishers. Used by permission. All rights reserved.

ISBN: 978-0-9816709-3-5

Contents

Acknowledgments

I want to thank God first and foremost. All of these pages are for His glory. I would also like to thank my family and friends for their love and support, and extend an extra special thank you to each person who willingly shared his or her testimony for inclusion in this book. It is those testimonies that inspired this book in the first place. I pray that the vulnerability and openness of those who shared will inspire spiritual transformation for someone else.

Introduction

Introduction

erhaps you've heard the expression "Into each life a little rain must fall." That's another way of saying that as long as we're alive, we can expect to have problems. While we may complain about the rain, especially when it interferes with our plans, we often forget that rain also benefits us. Without it, crops wouldn't break through the dry, hard ground; flowers wouldn't grow; and the earth's waters wouldn't be replenished. In the same way, trials are like rain for our souls. God's purpose for allowing suffering into our lives is good. It breaks up the hardness of our hearts, clears away the dirt of pride and stubbornness, and replenishes us so that beautiful things can grow in our lives.

When trials come, we tend to ask questions like, *Why did God allow this to happen? What have I done to deserve this? Where was God during this tragedy?* While such questions are normal, getting to know God on a deeply personal level can put many of them to rest. He has a greater purpose for our struggles than we may be able to see. Our trials are put into perspective when we begin to understand God's character and grasp the truth that everything He allows into our lives is a reflection of His love for us.

This book is not intended to help you avoid the storms of life. It is intended to help you discover God's greatness in the midst of them. When you're experiencing stormy weather, you need encouragement and motivation to go forward, knowing that God will never leave you nor forsake you (Hebrews 13:5). When the rain seems to wash away all you have, this book will help you look forward to the flowers the rain will soon produce. Their blossoms will be far more beautiful and fragrant than anything you could have ever known before.

No matter how great the purpose of the storm, however, rain is still rain, and it can leave you wet, cold, and frustrated. Perhaps your trial has been going on for a long time and you're struggling to keep your faith. Perhaps it looks as if there is no end in sight. Perhaps one problem hasn't even ended before another has overwhelmed you. Whatever your situation, God's Word has the answers you need. The Bible says, "The LORD is near to the brokenhearted and saves the crushed in spirit" (Psalm 34:18). Out of His deep compassion, God wants to wrap His arms around you, comfort you, and warm you with His love.

When you are struggling, it is easy to forget that God is ever present. Do you feel as though your Heavenly Father has abandoned you or that He doesn't care about your heartache? Nothing could be further from the truth. Scripture says, "He does not forget the cry of the afflicted" (Psalm 9:12). The God who created you knows you better than anyone else. Since He chose to make the ultimate sacrifice of His only Son for your sins, you can be sure that He doesn't view you or your struggles as insignificant. He understands you completely and loves you unconditionally. He can minister to you in ways no human being ever could.

The stories in these pages come from my own experiences and those of others. They are meant to encourage and remind you that no matter what kind of storm you encounter, there is hope. If God can work in the lives of others, He can work in your life as well. Nothing is too hard for Him. While His answers may be delayed, He desires to work through your circumstances for your good. Not only can He work in your circumstances, He wants to—and He will.

My prayer is that when the rain comes, you will be comforted in the midst of any pain and look forward to the fruit it will produce in your life and in the lives of those around you. May you know and experience to a greater degree the incredible depth of God's love for you.

1

Got Problems?

I love riding roller coasters. The excitement builds as you hear the *click, click, click* of the car inching its way to the top of the first hill. You look ahead to see what's coming and look down to watch the ground disappearing below you. As you crest the hill, you notice that the faces of the other riders reflect the same nervous anticipation. You wonder whether you will survive the ride and mentally calculate the laws of probability. When the car tilts from horizontal to vertical, screams fill the air. The car plummets toward the earth at breakneck speed, turns suddenly to the left and right, and loops upside down. Then comes another hill and the cycle begins again.

A roller coaster is a lot like life. Its thrilling highs and terrifying lows parallel the ups and downs we all experience. You may be thinking, *The difference between life and a roller coaster ride is that I know the roller coaster will ultimately deliver me safely back to the platform.* As believers, we have the same assurance. In John 16:33, Jesus tells us, "I have said these things to you, that in me you may have peace. In the world you will have tribulation. But take heart; I have overcome the world." Sometimes, overcoming the world means being delivered from trials. Other times, it means being preserved through them. Either way, we can take heart because whatever the path of the roller coaster, Jesus assures us that *in Him* we may have peace. In the end, He will deliver us to His chosen destination, whatever happens along the way. Because of that, we can have confidence about our destiny, even though we may feel afraid during the scary parts.

Denial: An Equal-Opportunity Destroyer

Because we are all human beings, we will experience suffering, tribulation, and pain. It doesn't matter whether we are young or old, single or married, atheist or Christian. At any point in time, each of us is coming out of a trial, in the middle of a trial, or getting ready to enter one. It is not a matter of *if* problems will come, but *when*.

How we respond to trials when they arise is critical. Many people deny their problems. They may seek distractions by losing themselves in romance, sleep, drugs, or alcohol. Some look for comfort in food, while others starve themselves to numb the pain. Workaholics avoid their problems by scheduling every minute of the day. Others find escape in social media, surfing the Internet, texting, shopping, exercising, playing video games, or watching television. While there is nothing wrong with these things in themselves, when misused, they can become ways of living in denial.

Think of denial as stuffing your pockets with the problems you don't want to face. The goal is to pretend everything is fine, but eventually, your pockets become so full that the seams begin to tear. As they do, your feelings leak out as raw, unprocessed emotions. When the pockets rip off completely, you experience overwhelming chaos as the stuffed emotions flood out uncontrollably.

Avoiding your problems does not make them go away. In fact, it fuels them by making them even bigger later on. As a Christian counselor, I often have to peel away the layers of my clients' emotions to get to the source of their hurt. Healing occurs at the root of the problems, but it doesn't come from my psychological insight or anyone else's. God is the only one who can truly heal, and He walks through the process with us hand in hand.

Do You Want to Be Well?

The Lord doesn't force us to change. We must make the choice to be well. In John 5:6, Jesus asked a man who had been an invalid for thirty-eight years if he wanted to be healed. While this might seem like a silly question, sadly some people are more comfortable in their illness than they think they would be in wellness.

If we refuse to turn to the Great Healer, we will seek out distractions as a way to get through our problems. For example, some people may state that they don't want to be alcoholics, but because of stress in their lives, they need to drink to get by. This, of course, isn't true. Alcohol may seem like a quick fix, but it only makes things worse. Depending on a substance rather than on God causes people to experience greater dissatisfaction, widening the gap between their current lives and the lives they truly want to live. Alcohol and other fillers might numb us to pain and problems temporarily, but the issues at the heart of our anguish only fester and grow.

Too often we want quick and immediate answers. Today's American culture demands instant gratification, and we want our pain to end immediately regardless of the cost. Rather than finding a successful way *through* our problems, we simply want a way *out*.

God allows us to go through trials in order to teach us valuable principles that will serve us well in the future. We can experience peace and comfort in the midst of our problems if we are open to His plan. Sometimes, like small children who are angry with their parents, we cross our arms, pout, and turn away from God, refusing any spiritual refreshment. We focus on the trial rather than on the lesson, and then become bitter or overwhelmed. When all we can see is the problem, this is what Scripture calls "walking by sight" (2 Corinthians 5:7). When we get to the point at which we can relax our arms and open them to God, He wraps His arms around us and fills our being with His peace. In that process, we mature and become more like Christ. The Father/child relationship deepens as our trust grows and we walk by faith with Jesus.

If you are experiencing a trial, God may be using it to shift your focus from you and your problem to Him and His solution. His goal is to teach you to depend on Him. Trusting Him means bringing His wisdom—not yours—to the table because He is the only One who can make sense of things.

The Bitter Fruit of Sin

We were never meant to go it alone. From the beginning, God wanted His creation to depend on Him for everything. He designed human beings to know Him and be known by Him in a relationship of comfortable intimacy. As we acknowledge His authority over us and learn to fully trust Him, we begin to recognize how He generously provides for our needs. But when we distance ourselves from God, we become blinded to His abundant provision. The separation and distance that developed between man and God was man's doing, not God's.

In the Garden of Eden, everything was pristine, including Adam and Eve's submission to God's sovereignty. There was only one rule they had to follow: "And the LORD God commanded the man, saying, 'You may surely eat of every tree of the garden, but of the tree of the knowledge of good and evil you shall not eat, for in the day that you eat of it you shall surely die'" (Genesis 2:16–17). God clearly warned Adam and Eve about the consequences of disobedience. They disobeyed Him anyway:

> But the serpent said to the woman, "You will not surely die. For God knows that when you eat of it your eyes will be opened, and you will be like God, knowing good and evil." So when the woman saw that the tree was good for food, and that it was a delight to the eyes, and that the tree was to be desired to make one wise, she took of its fruit and ate, and she also

gave some to her husband who was with her, and he ate. Then the eyes of both were opened, and they knew that they were naked. And they sewed fig leaves together and made themselves loincloths. (Genesis 3:4–7)

At face value, there was nothing wrong with Eve's desire. After all, what could be wrong with wanting to be wise? The problem was that God had forbidden Adam and Eve to eat from that tree. Eve, however, reasoned that there was nothing wrong with her desires because her intentions were good. Therefore, she thought God was withholding something they deserved. She took control of the situation and attempted to fix the *perceived* problem by taking what she wanted. After she bit into the fruit, I believe she immediately realized what she had done was wrong. I think she tried to assuage her guilt by getting Adam to take a bite too, thereby justifying her action (like our modern excuse of "Everybody is doing it!"). Instead of obeying God's command, Adam took the forbidden fruit Eve offered him, joining her in disobedience. Adam and Eve's attempt to sidestep their guilt did not work, and they both knew they had disobeyed God. Rather than going to Him and confessing their wrongdoing, they sewed fig leaves into coverings to hide their nakedness. The problem started when Adam and Eve left God's fellowship, believing lies about Him. It continued when they disobeyed His command by eating the fruit. Then they avoided the obvious solution of returning to God, humbling themselves, and asking forgiveness. They chose to hide instead.

This is what Christians call "the fall," the entry of human sin into the world. As a result of Adam and Eve's disobedience, all human beings have been born with a sinful nature and must deal with pain, suffering, and death (Genesis 3:16–19; Romans 5:12–13). Moreover, Adam and Eve's actions did not affect them alone. They affected all of creation (Romans 8:22). We continue to follow them in disobedience, each of us sinning in our own ways (Romans 3:23).

The disastrous consequences of the fall can only be removed by God Himself. If we will understand that God wants the best for us and allow Him to wash away our sin by accepting His forgiveness through the cross, God will show us His power and grace because He alone can reconcile us to Himself by removing our pride and guilt.

In our culture, we are taught that independence is the key to success. However, this mentality tempts us to live independently of God too. Independence from God is a hindrance to our faith and ability to submit to His will for our lives. Jesus depended on the Father for everything (John 5:19).

What's your initial reaction when troubles arise? Do you try to figure out how to fix your problems based solely on your own skills and abilities? Or do you look to God for help and wisdom? If you depend on yourself for answers, how is that working out for you? Our resources are limited, but God's are unlimited. What will it take for you to stop relying on yourself and turn to God, seeking His truth and wisdom instead?

Two Choices

When faced with a problem, we can respond by becoming bitter or becoming better. Some people emerge bitter. They become grumpy, difficult, and perpetually angry. They have trouble relating to others and often isolate themselves. They are unpleasant to be around, and no one enjoys their company. These people are unteachable, thinking they have all the answers. With this attitude, they are doomed to repeat the same mistakes over and over. Others emerge better, coming through their struggles joyful, content, and thankful. They learn and grow from their trials and are able to help others who face similar problems. These people are a joy to be around, and others flock to them.

Which kind of person do you want to be? If you can keep your heart from responding to your problems with rebellion and bitterness, and if you desire to have a teachable spirit, you will be able to feel the touch of God. On the other hand, if you harden your heart, you will wrap yourself in a shell so hard that even God's tender ministrations will not penetrate. In the process, you will hinder your growth.

Sometimes we feel overwhelmed by the enormity of the challenges we face, and overcoming them seems like more than we can bear. When we feel this way, we often cannot see God because we're too blinded by our own points of view. Ironically, that perspective can limit God's work in our lives. The next time you face a trial that you think will break you, remember that God loves you, and every trial you face is filtered through His loving hands. He allows trials into your life to accomplish specific purposes that He intends to benefit you from an eternal perspective.

Throughout this book, each chapter contains the story of a person who has endured trials and overcome them, ultimately coming to see and better understand the love of the Father as a result. You, too, may find that God will give you peace when you trust Him to work in your situation. In order for God to move mountains on your behalf, however, you have to give Him control.

A Reason for
All Seasons

*B*ecause of the original sin committed by Adam and Eve, mankind now faces heartache and sorrow. God is not vindictive. He has good reasons for allowing us to experience pain. When I consider the teaching of the Bible and the character of God, I can think of at least four reasons God allows us to experience difficulties. We will discuss them throughout this chapter.

Whether God's aim is to work in your life, to impact someone else's life through you, or both, the truth is that God uses painful circumstances for good purposes. The more clearly we understand this truth, the richer our lives will become. Let's take a closer look at four divine "reasons for difficult seasons" and see if any of them ring true in your experience.

Reason #1:
To Reveal God's Majesty

God uses the trials of life to display His sovereignty, His glory, and His power. Many disasters around the world have focused our attention on spiritual things. God works the same way in us as individuals. When personal tragedies occur, our priorities shift, and the desire for answers, peace, and comfort turn us to God.

Likewise, when we experience seemingly tragic events and see God accomplishing great things through them, we are drawn to Him.

Consider Peter's seemingly desperate situation in Acts 12. He was imprisoned, chained to guards, and scheduled for execution. By any rational criteria, the situation seemed hopeless. However, God responded to Peter's plight in the best way to advance His kingdom purposes. He sent an angel to open the prison gates, woke up Peter, and set him free. Peter then went to the house where other believers were praying for him, revealing God's miraculous answer to their prayers. What an encouraging account!

Everyone who has read this passage can see how God is involved in the lives of individual people, doing great things for them. As a result, many have chosen to follow God and experience more of His goodness themselves. Although God doesn't always choose to answer our prayers with such quick and miraculous action, we know He is capable of revealing His power in every area of our lives at any time.

Reason #2:
To Teach Us Something

As a loving Father, God uses our helplessness to teach us to trust Him, develop deeper faith, and bring us to spiritual maturity. God cares about us so much that He wants to mature us as believers in Christ.

Each battle we face can be used for growth and maturity. There are always lessons to learn as we struggle through problems and issues. These lessons are what mold us into the person God created us to be. It's like playing a video game in which you learn the ins and outs of each play in order to reach the next level. It takes practice and sometimes making the wrong moves to learn the right moves toward victory.

We see this in the life of Mary Magdalene. Mary struggled with low self-esteem, a sinful lifestyle, and the presence of evil spirits

(Luke 8). These problems led her to Jesus. In Him, she felt loved and valued for the first time in her life. Through Him, she made friends with other godly women. As Mary Magdalene served Jesus, her trust and faith grew. But her life-changing battle came at the cross. She was present for Jesus' scourging, trial, and crucifixion. Witnessing His agonizing death shook her to the core, but she stayed with Jesus the whole time. Three days later, Mary went to Jesus' tomb to anoint His body. When she arrived, Jesus was gone. Mary believed someone had stolen His body. Even when Jesus appeared to her, she didn't recognize Him. Yet when He spoke her name, she remembered Jesus' teachings that He would rise from the dead. Through this painful experience, Mary saw Jesus for who He really is: God incarnate, omnipotent, faithful, and trustworthy.

God is not unaware of our suffering. Rather, He uses it to move us from one level of spiritual maturity to another.

Reason #3:
To Allow Us to Experience Consequences

Sometimes God permits problems into our lives so we will experience the consequences of our sin, foolishness, and immaturity. We sin when we make a choice that goes against God's will. When we turn away from God's plan, we walk away from His protection and into His discipline. Sometimes He spares us from the immediate consequences of our actions. Other times He allows us to experience at least part of what we deserve.

King David is considered one of the greatest heroes of the Bible. God called him a man after His own heart (Acts 13:22). Yet David sometimes succumbed to sin and suffered the consequences, including the death of his son. But as a man after God's own heart, King David came to recognize the consequences of his sin and repented. He said:

O LORD, rebuke me not in your anger, nor discipline me in your wrath! For your arrows have sunk into me, and your hand has come down on me. There is no soundness in my flesh because of your indignation; there is no health in my bones because of my sin. For my iniquities have gone over my head; like a heavy burden, they are too heavy for me. My wounds stink and fester because of my foolishness, I am utterly bowed down and prostrate; all the day I go about mourning. For my sides are filled with burning, and there is no soundness in my flesh. I am feeble and crushed; I groan because of the tumult of my heart. (Psalm 38:1–8)

God created us to be in fellowship with Him, so we suffer when that harmony is broken. As King David discovered, we may not always anticipate just how much damage our sin will cause. The consequences of our sin are greater than we imagine. When people engage in premarital sex, for example, they don't take seriously the possibility of bringing a sexually transmitted disease into their future marriage. We often believe that we will somehow avoid the negative results of our actions.

The Bible is our guidebook for how to live a life that honors God. We are called to be holy just as God is holy (1 Peter 1:16). If we step outside His guidelines, there is a price to pay. This is not to punish us, but to teach us. By giving us a guidebook, God is not trying to take away our joy. He is trying to maximize our joy and protect us. Sometimes it takes looking back on the consequences of our poor choices to teach us the benefit of future obedience. As hard as the lessons may be, our struggles teach us that God always has our best interests at heart.

Not all consequences arise because of deliberate sin. Sometimes they are the result of foolishness or immaturity. Take, for instance, people who want to experience financial freedom but aren't willing to do what's required to achieve it. They spend foolishly, buy things they don't need, and max out their credit cards, only to wonder why they are struggling to make ends meet. In these cases, God may use circumstances to get their attention. He may allow some people to lose their homes to show them they need to be financially responsible. It's not that God caused this to happen. It is a consequence of their poor financial decisions. God allows such consequences, as painful as they are, because He wants His children to learn how to use money wisely and live in peace, not in bondage.

Even seemingly good things, like dedication to your job or church activities, can cause problems if there is spiritual or emotional immaturity in your life. For example, choosing to work ten extra hours each week to earn more money for a fancy car or family vacation can be a good thing, but if that overtime causes you to miss your children's soccer games or date nights with your spouse, your family relationships can suffer.

Reason #4:
To Benefit the Lives of Others

Sometimes God allows us to undergo trials in order to use us as instruments in the lives of others. Our main role as Christians is to bring people closer to God. However, that may not always feel like a blessing. Many have suffered through illness, injury, or debilitating pain even as they sought to serve God. Although no one would willingly choose such experiences, God can use a person's place of suffering to minister to others. Christians who have endured physical anguish can give others hope that there is peace and eternal healing through a relationship with God.

The Apostle Paul suffered repeatedly throughout his ministry. He told the church at Corinth that because of what he and his co-laborers suffered, they were better able to encourage the church in their struggles. He wrote, "Blessed be the God and Father of our Lord Jesus Christ, the Father of mercies and God of all comfort, who comforts us in all our affliction, so that we may be able to comfort those who are in any affliction, with the comfort with which we ourselves are comforted by God" (2 Corinthians 1:3–4). Paul's suffering demonstrates that God is the source of all things, including comfort. He wouldn't have been able to show that comfort unless he struggled himself. His response to suffering made a difference to the Corinthians as it does for us today.

In cases of alcoholism, abuse, or adultery, children can become emotionally or physically wounded by the lifestyle of their parents. Those sins can cause a chain reaction of pain and destruction. But with God's redemptive power, even those experiences can be used to minister to others who are hurting. As God brings comfort and healing to those hurts, we can bring hope to others in similar situations. God can use those areas of healing to let others know they are not alone. We can embrace them with the message, "As God was with me, I am with you, and He is with you also."

Of course, you don't have to be hurting in order to positively impact the lives of those around you. When you sacrifice your time to help out at a soup kitchen, when you hear of a family that is struggling and take them a meal, or when you bake a birthday cake for a child who doesn't have a stable family, you are showing God's love in a way they may not have experienced before. God will often use your kindness to draw people to Himself. We may voluntarily suffer hardship to give sacrificially, but what is only a small sacrifice (or even a joy) for us can be a big blessing to someone else.

When people are hurting, simple acts of kindness can do so much. Reaching out and developing relationships with people is a sure way to make an impact. God will use you to reach the hearts of others, mold them, and help them mature spiritually.

Satan's Tactics

We can learn from our troubles if we accept responsibility and don't try to pass the blame. "Passing the buck" has been around since the dawn of time. Adam and Eve blamed each other, Satan, and even God. In Genesis 3:11–13 God said, "'Who told you that you were naked? Have you eaten of the tree of which I commanded you not to eat?' The man said, 'The woman whom you gave to be with me, she gave me fruit of the tree, and I ate.' Then the LORD God said to the woman, 'What is this that you have done?' The woman said, 'The serpent deceived me, and I ate.'" We find it easier to blame someone else than to take responsibility for our actions.

Sometimes, such as when a tornado demolishes our home or we lose a job through downsizing, we have not been the cause of our problems. However, if we have played a role, God wants us to take responsibility for the role we've played in our own suffering and allow Him to work in our circumstances to help us grow through them. The Bible says, "Be sober-minded; be watchful. Your adversary the devil prowls around like a roaring lion, seeking someone to devour" (1 Peter 5:8). Sometimes instead of examining ourselves, we let Satan persuade us to redirect the blame.

Other times, Satan's strategy is more subtle. He may exhaust us so we are too tired and overwhelmed to deal with the issues at hand. How often do we try so hard to keep our heads above water and stay ahead of the bills that we say, "I don't have time to pray about these things"? When we make this excuse, we forget that God is our Provider. The Psalmist wrote, "It is in vain that you rise up early and go late to rest, eating the bread of anxious toil; for he gives to his beloved sleep" (Psalm 127:2). When we focus on God and seek to live out His will for our lives, He will meet our needs (Matthew 6:19–33).

In the midst of trials, our focus should not be on working harder to fix them. It should be on trusting God, seeking Him, and allowing Him to work out the details. When we don't take the time to pray, read the Scriptures, and seek God's wisdom in what He wants us to learn or how He wants us to grow, we are playing right into Satan's hands. We reject God's provision and sovereignty and fail to wield the strongest weapons we have—faith and prayer.

Learn from Others' Trials

We don't have to experience a trial ourselves in order to learn the lessons God wants to teach us. God may choose to protect us from disaster by allowing us to see consequences in the lives of others. For example, Kyle worked for a big corporation. One day he saw his coworker, Jeff, taking some office supplies home for personal use. Jeff reasoned that the company had so much that they wouldn't notice a few things missing. One day Jeff was called into the boss's office and was fired for theft. This was a timely lesson for Kyle, who had considered doing the same thing. Kyle was glad he chose not to follow Jeff's example. He learned from another's mistake instead of repeating it.

Why don't we learn from the experiences of others more often? Sometimes it is because we deny the possibility that bad things will ever happen to us. When people are driving and think about sending a quick text message, they don't typically imagine losing concentration and getting into a terrible accident. They only think about the compelling desire to communicate. People who operate with this mindset are usually shocked when bad things happen because they think they're somehow immune. The more mature response is to think through the unintended consequences. *Bad things are more likely to happen to me if I'm not careful. What can I do to prevent them?* This approach sets up a barrier of protection around us because we are consciously guarding ourselves from trouble instead of jumping in headfirst and dealing with any painful consequences later.

Life Lessons

We tend to think it is easier to ignore our problems than to deal with them, but life doesn't work that way. If we disregard the lessons God is trying to teach us, we will end up dealing with the same problems again and again. I have counseled many women who suffered at the hands of abusive husbands, divorced them, and turned around only to marry men just like them. God's plan is to help us learn certain lessons, but we will end up repeating our mistakes if we miss the lessons the first time. When we're tempted to ignore a problem because it is too difficult or painful to face, we should ask ourselves, *Is this a lesson I want to repeat? Is this a problem I want to go through again?*

Confronting challenges doesn't have to be a frightening experience. The One who created you knows you inside and out. He cares about every detail of your life. Psalm 37:23–24 reminds us, "The steps of a man are established by the LORD, when he delights in his way; though he fall, he shall not be cast headlong, for the LORD upholds his hand." You can trust your future to God. His plans are ultimately for your good because He loves you as a father adores his little child.

A friend shared with me a wonderful reflection on being secure in God's love and remaining there even when faced with adversity. She said, "When I was little, my dad was crazy about me and proud as a peacock of every little thing I did. This is what a father is supposed to do. Every day when he came home from work, he threw out his arms and said, 'How's my baby? Come to Daddy!' His eyes lit up with joy just to see me. I laughed and ran into his arms, and he lifted me to his chest so I could hear his heart beating. He snuggled me to his neck and kissed me. I never for an instant doubted his love. I could trust him no matter what I might be going through. Even at the age of three, I knew I was safe in his arms and everything would be all right."

That is an amazing picture of love, yet it is only a glimmer of how God feels about us. God loves us more than any human father ever could. He treasures and cherishes us, and every trial is filtered through His loving hands. He allows those trials into our lives, and no matter how awful they may seem, they are part of His perfect plan for us. So why do we doubt God's love when something goes wrong? Instead of being upset at the pain we are suffering, we can accept the embrace of God as we climb into His lap, confident of His great love for us. God is a proud Papa who dotes on His little ones. What a precious thing to know that God is crazy about us!

Nancy's Story

The following is a powerful testimony from my friend Nancy, who was once overwhelmed by heartache and depression. This story shows that bad things can happen to good people, but they happen for a purpose. I hope that seeing how God worked through her difficult season can encourage you in your own struggles.

I grew up in a loving Christian home, but because of the perfectionist views of my mother and my church, I had unrealistic expectations. I expected myself to be perfect, and nothing else would do. Even as a small child, I did my best to never complain and to always cooperate and obey. But I did it out of my flesh, trying to please God and make Him love me more, as if that were possible.

It wasn't until I was an adult that I realized what an unhealthy view of the world this was. No matter how hard I tried, I wasn't perfect. My attitudes and thoughts certainly weren't holy, and regardless of how much effort I put into things, I still missed the mark and struggled to accept myself for who I was. I would go to church every week and confess my sins, but I would leave still carrying the same terrible load. I would read the Scriptures and wonder, *If this is all true, why don't I feel victorious and free? What's wrong with me?*

When I was in my thirties, I experienced loss after loss, beginning with the deaths of my mother and beloved grandmother. The struggles continued with my dad's brain injury and disability, a house fire, a miscarriage, and several other devastating experiences. They left me reeling, wondering what I had done to deserve such heartache.

My mother taught me that bad things never happen to good people. This only reinforced my feelings of inadequacy. Over time, I fell into a deep clinical depression and could not escape the pain. Desperate to stop the emotional turmoil, I made a plan to end my life.

One beautiful September day, I took my children to school, went home, cleaned the house, put supper in the fridge and future meals in the freezer, cleaned up loose ends, and made a list for my husband to carry on in my absence.

I drove to a nearby city, pulled into a parking lot, and waited for the next train. Colorful leaves wafted through the air on the wings of the wind. The air was fragrant with the smell of burning leaves, all signs of my favorite time of year. I scarcely noticed because my pain was so intense.

Soon I heard the sound of the train and felt the vibration of the wheels thundering down the track. I drove my car to where the tracks intersected the parking lot, planning to drive in front of the train just before it arrived.

I wept as I told the Lord that I didn't really want to die, but I couldn't go on this way anymore. I said, "Lord, in my pain I can't seem to feel Your presence or hear Your voice, so if You have any last words, please speak to me now."

Abruptly, light and heat filled the passenger seat beside me. God's presence filled the car. He said, "This isn't My plan for you, My dove. I have so much more for you to do—things beyond your wildest dreams."

I wept even harder as I said, "All I need to know is that You haven't abandoned me." Overcome with relief, I turned my car around and headed home, knowing God loved and cherished me. At home, I sat at my desk, wrote down all the things that were too much to bear (two hundred pages in all), then burned them. At that point, the Lord lifted the load and carried it off on angels' wings, never to haunt me again.

In that process, I learned that no matter how heavy the burden or how awful the pain, God is there. Although we may feel alone, He is merely waiting on us to get into that secret place of intimacy where we can let Him take the pain from our shoulders, wrap us in His loving embrace, and wipe away our tears. He will restore our hope and joy and give us a reason to live.

Through this experience, I finally understood that bad things do happen to good people. When they happen, God is there to love and encourage us. I now understand that whatever I lack, He is. He completes me. Because of Him, I am accepted in the Beloved, never inadequate in His eyes. No wonder the Psalmist said, "Let them thank the LORD for his steadfast love, for his wondrous works to the children of man!" (Psalm 107:31).

If Nancy had ended her life, she never would have experienced the incredible joy and blessing God had planned for her on the far side of her suffering. Since being lifted from her depression, Nancy has used her new perspective and sense of purpose to write nearly thirty Christian books that lift up and glorify God. She describes her new life as being "filled to overflowing, knowing that just when it seems as if all is lost, God has wonderful things around the corner if we'll just hang on and not give up."

Trials Aren't
Wasted Time

*S*ome people think that by putting their faith in God, they should be able to pray away their trials. When their suffering and pain don't go away, they might ask, "Why is this happening, God?" When that question goes unanswered, they may turn their backs on God, believing He has turned His back on them. While problems ultimately serve a purpose for our spiritual good, they may test our faith and shake us to our core.

If anyone deserved to feel as if God had abandoned or forgotten him, it was Joseph. His story of betrayal, suffering, and ultimate redemption is told in Genesis. As a young man, Joseph had lofty dreams and plans. After all, God had given him a vision of his future—that people would bow down to him, even his own family. Then Joseph found himself a slave and a prisoner. That's not the way the plan was supposed to go!

Jacob, Joseph's father, made it no secret that Joseph was his favorite son. When Jacob gave him a wonderful coat of many colors, Joseph's ten brothers were consumed by jealousy and formulated a plan to get rid of him. One day, they captured Joseph, threw him into a pit, shredded his coat, and covered it with animal's blood. Then they told their father that his favorite son was dead. At the first opportunity, the brothers sold Joseph as a slave to a passing caravan.

Unbeknownst to the brothers, they could not disrupt God's purpose. God still had plans for Joseph. Joseph was taken to Egypt and sold to Potiphar, one of Pharaoh's officials. The Lord gave Joseph favor in the eyes of his master, and Potiphar trusted him with running the entire household.

Joseph was a handsome man, however, and Potiphar's wife wanted to sleep with him. He refused the sinful enticement, but Potiphar's wife wouldn't take no for an answer. One day she cornered him. Joseph continued to refuse her advances and ran off, leaving behind his cloak. The scorned woman told her husband that Joseph had attacked her, and Potiphar put Joseph in prison. Talk about a confidence-shattering turn of events!

Wait! The story isn't over. While Joseph was incarcerated, he met Pharaoh's cupbearer and his baker, both of whom had been imprisoned for offending their leader. When they learned that Joseph could analyze dreams from God, they asked him what their dreams meant. Joseph provided the interpretation of each dream, predicting that the baker would be hung for his offenses while the cupbearer would soon get out of prison and be restored to his former position. Joseph asked the cupbearer to put in a good word with Pharaoh after he was released.

Joseph's interpretations were shown to be true. The baker was hanged and the cupbearer was freed, but despite Joseph's request, the cupbearer forgot to mention Joseph to Pharaoh. Even then, all was not lost. Sometime later, when Pharaoh couldn't understand the meaning of one of his dreams, the cupbearer remembered Joseph and told Pharaoh what Joseph had done for him.

Pharaoh called Joseph out of prison to interpret his dream. God showed Joseph that Pharaoh's dream was a warning. For the next seven years, there would be a great harvest in the land of Egypt.

This time of bounty would be followed by seven years of severe famine. The country would only survive if the harvest from the seven years of abundance was properly managed.

Deeply impressed, Pharaoh chose Joseph for the job. He made Joseph his right-hand man, second in command only to Pharaoh himself. Because of Joseph's faithful service, countless people were saved from starvation.

Among those seeking relief from the famine were Jacob's family. When the older brothers went to Pharaoh to buy food, they found Joseph instead. At first they didn't recognize him, but ultimately, the relationship between the brothers was restored. Joseph was able to reunite with his entire family.

What Joseph's brothers did was evil, but God used their wrong choices for His good purpose. God never left Joseph's side. He continually showed him favor even when it did not look like it. Joseph had times of suffering, but his life was ultimately one of abundance. God used him to save his family and countless others. Joseph recognized this and later told his brothers, "As for you, you meant evil against me, but God meant it for good, to bring it about that many people should be kept alive, as they are today" (Genesis 50:20). God also used the experience to bring his brothers to repentance and heal their relationship with him.

Trials don't happen because of God's lack of love for us. The opposite is true. Trials happen because He loves us. It may be hard to accept, but God allows us to suffer for our benefit and the benefit of those around us. While we may not understand the reasons for the challenges we face this side of heaven, God's goal is for us to learn and grow through them.

Like Joseph, you might experience rejection, disappointment, unfairness, cruelty, or seemingly hopeless circumstances. Like him, you may experience years of tragedies or delays. Know that just as God worked through Joseph's circumstances, He can also work through yours. Through his suffering, Joseph remained faithful to God. God not only protected Joseph through the trouble, He also used his trials to bring about purposes that only His sovereignty could foresee.

Take a lesson from the life of Joseph. Don't become bitter or let impatience steal your faith that God's good purposes will prevail. God has His hand in everything that happens to us. You may have heard that some people come into our lives for a season and some for a reason. When it comes to trials, both are true. Problems come for a season, and God permits them for a reason—because He loves us.

What Is Your Focus?

The fastest way to become overwhelmed by a problem is to focus on the problem rather than on God. When you question why God is allowing you to suffer, you can spend an inordinate amount of time and energy trying to make sense of it all. Ultimately, this will make the problem seem even bigger and more difficult.

Like holding on to a heavy anchor, too much pondering on your past can drag you down and drown you in your sorrows. Many people wish they had done something differently or that things had worked out another way. They become so consumed by what could have been that they stop hoping for what might be.

When you get behind the wheel of a car, you should spend the majority of your time looking forward to see where you are going. If you are constantly looking in the rearview mirror, you will inevitably have a wreck. The same principle applies to life. It is always best to look ahead. This doesn't mean we should disregard the past and the lessons we can learn from it, but we shouldn't spend so much time looking back that we fail to see what's coming down the road.

If you look beyond your problems and focus on God, your burdens will become lighter. In Matthew 11:28–30, Jesus says, "Come to me, all who labor and are heavy laden, and I will give you rest. Take my yoke upon you, and learn from me, for I am gentle and lowly in heart, and you will find rest for your souls. For my yoke is easy, and my burden is light." A yoke is a frame that fits over a person's shoulders to balance heavy loads. People carry emotional yokes too. Those who have heavy burdens in their hearts and souls are weighed down by internal strain. If we choose to allow God to work through our situations and exchange our yokes with Him, our burdens will be lighter and life will be a lot less stressful.

Learning to Wait

One of the ways to wait patiently for God to work out the details of your trial is to remind yourself, *This too shall pass.* It is easy to become frustrated when we are looking at a problem from the beginning or when we are only partway through. Things often look very different once we're on the other side!

A few years ago, I was invited to attend a weekend conference and was told that it would be life changing. I thought it was a Christian conference. To my surprise, it was secular, and the leaders implemented group and individual exercises to bring out past hurts in order to let individuals express their feelings about them. The goal was self-sufficiency. I couldn't identify a biblical foundation or even a healthy secular basis for the protocol. Nevertheless, I participated in the activities and witnessed others doing the same. Instead of feeling better, I left the weekend with confusion, bitterness, and hatred toward others.

When I arrived home, I realized that the disorientation I felt was due to the fact that I had not given my struggles to God during the conference. The worldly advice did nothing to correct my problems or alleviate my emotional pain.

True empowerment does not come from expressing our feelings to others. It comes when we surrender to God and submit to His will. He wants us to be healed of past wounds and to forgive those who have hurt us. We can be restored only when we turn our problems over to God. The Psalmist says, "He heals the brokenhearted and binds up their wounds" (Psalm 147:3).

God helped me work through the negative feelings stirred up after that weekend. I prayed through the issues, forgave those who had caused me pain, and meditated on scriptural truths. This experience taught me two lessons. The first is that, to succeed through trials, I must focus on my relationship with God, expressing my frustrations and hurts to Him, and asking Him for the strength to make it through. I need to seek the faith to trust His sovereignty. Second, although I initially thought the conference was a waste of time and had a negative impact on my life, in the end, it turned out for my good. It surfaced pain from past experiences that I had not seen before and helped me realize that all pain, past and present, should direct me to God.

While we may not always see how a particular struggle could possibly serve a greater purpose, someday we will understand. Paul writes, "For now we see in a mirror dimly, but then face to face. Now I know in part; then I shall know fully, even as I have been fully known" (1 Corinthians 13:12). How comforting! It is hard to understand why God allows suffering, especially if we have done nothing to cause it. However, the Bible promises that someday all things will be made clear. Until then, we rest in faith.

Could you live in peace during long seasons of suffering, trusting that God is working all things together for good even though you cannot see it at the time? If Jesus' yoke is easy and His burden is light, why is it so hard for us to turn our problems over to Him? We may sing "I Surrender All" with great conviction, but when trials come, we often fail to surrender. We may say, "God is in control," but deep down we think we can run our lives better than He can. We may take steps to try to remedy a difficult situation, but when those steps are not part of God's plan, they can move us further away from the real solution.

It is only natural to question our circumstances. However, once we realize that God has allowed those circumstances into our lives and we make the choice to surrender control to Him, life's challenges become easier to accept. Surrender results in spiritual maturity. God uses problems to help us grow in our faith, but He never leaves us on our own.

Paul's Experience with Grace

Even the heroes of the Bible were not immune to suffering. In fact, the most godly men and women in Scripture seemed to suffer the most. The Apostle Paul, who wrote the majority of the New Testament, wrote about an unidentified "thorn" in his flesh. This thorn must have been exceedingly painful, whether physically or emotionally, because Paul prayed three times for God to remove it. God's choice was not to remove the thorn. Instead, He gave Paul revelation about the reason for the suffering. Paul writes,

> So to keep me from becoming conceited because of the surpassing greatness of the revelations, a thorn was given me in the flesh, a messenger of Satan to harass me, to keep me from becoming conceited. Three times I pleaded with the Lord about this, that it should leave me. But he said to me, "My grace is sufficient for you, for my power is made perfect in weakness." Therefore I will boast all the more gladly of my weaknesses, so that the power of Christ may rest upon me. For the sake of Christ, then, I am content with weaknesses, insults, hardships, persecutions, and calamities. For when I am weak, then I am strong. (2 Corinthians 12:7–10)

God had revealed certain things to Paul that were too great to write down. That would inflate anyone's ego, wouldn't it? This passage suggests that the thorn was intended to keep Paul from becoming conceited. We are not told what this thorn was or how it would accomplish this purpose, but Paul's response was to humble himself and submit to God's sovereignty. Not many of us would respond to hardship with such submission. Paul knew that learning to trust God is one of the main purposes for trials. Likewise, God may not change the difficult situation you are facing if that is what it takes to accomplish His will. However, He will change you *through* your circumstances if you allow Him to do so.

Only God can see the whole picture of how our lives will play out. Our responsibility is to wait, and through the process of waiting, learn to trust Him more. Although we may not understand it, His plan is always perfect.

Kim's Story

Let's look at the testimony of a dear woman who experienced the heartache of abortion. Her transgression resulted in years of pain and guilt, but when she sought genuine forgiveness, she discovered the fullness of God's love and unconditional acceptance. Her story demonstrates how God uses our struggles for purposes we cannot even fathom.

I was engaged in my early twenties when I learned to my shock that I was pregnant. I was three months into a radio career in Minneapolis, which I considered a rare and precious second chance since I had dropped out of college four years earlier. At that time, my parents had been divorced for a year and were unable to provide financial support, so I was on my own. Determined not to fail, I had made up my mind to be independent and make my own way, but I was completely unprepared when my fiancé refused to marry me or support the child.

I was devastated. How could I take care of myself, establish a career, and be a single parent at the same time? It seemed impossible. On top of that, I was ashamed of having been sexually active before marriage.

There was a deeper issue as well. Appearance meant everything to me. I had always tried to do things to earn the love and respect of others but ended up using them to get what I wanted. I never let anyone get too close. I was lost, but I didn't know it. While I looked competent and successful on the outside, I was empty and lonely on the inside. I was deeply afraid of criticism and rejection. I constantly struggled with feelings of inferiority. I never felt good enough.

The day of the abortion is a bit like a dream now. At the time, it felt like sleepwalking. I was already a master at detaching from my feelings, so I steeled myself to get through it. I was determined to forget it completely once it was over. I kept my head down through the whole process, trying not to speak or make eye contact with anyone.

Even now, I cannot remember most of the details of what took place. For years, I couldn't even recall the season of the year. But one thing stands out very clearly. The woman helping with the procedure took my hand and offered words of comfort. Her actions broke through my detachment enough to shock me into reality. In that moment, I knew that what I was about to do was wrong, yet I didn't have the strength of character to say, "Stop!" Instead, I lay there and let it happen.

A very long time passed before I could face the reality of what I had done. I sometimes held my own hand, trying to recall that bit of kindness the woman at the clinic had shown me. It didn't help.

I was distraught about the abortion and the truth regarding my fiancé's values. We split up a few months later.

One of the so-called benefits of abortion is that no one needs to know. However, you soon find that your secret holds you captive. I told myself my parents would be disappointed, a new boyfriend or future husband would never forgive me, and, of course, I would never in a million years admit it to my future children. Even though I had been raised in the church, I didn't really know Jesus, so there was no help there.

Several years after the abortion, I got married. My husband and I had two beautiful children. Though we attended church, I was no closer to salvation. The marriage failed eight years later, a casualty of emotional baggage and the absence of Christ.

I finally came to the end of myself. Completely broken, I began attending a twelve-step group. There I met a woman who saw something good in me. Whenever I expressed guilt or despair, she would say, "Kim, Jesus loves you, and as soon as you confess your sins, you are forgiven." She said it so often that I found myself meditating on that promise. In April 1990, the Holy Spirit opened my eyes to the meaning of Jesus' sacrifice, and I finally believed and became a Christian.

Later I remarried, and God gradually brought me along in my spiritual walk. It didn't come quickly, but step by step He helped me to understand the true freedom I could experience in Christ. Through God's gentle guidance, I learned to stop seeing Him as Judge and began to see Him as a gentle Shepherd who loves to restore His beloved.

One day I realized how I had allowed my guilt to keep me from the full love and unconditional acceptance of God. I fell to my knees and said, "Jesus, I understand. I'm so sorry." At that moment, I felt His love washing over me as I accepted His precious gift of mercy. All the guilt, self-doubt, pride, and hurt simply fell away. A lifetime of pain was healed in the time it took to say a few words.

Today I live a life of freedom. By God's grace and through the support of the godly women God has placed around me, I have been able to forgive each person who had any part in the loss of my child. I have also accepted God's forgiveness for the part I played.

God has redeemed my career by giving me a Christian outreach to help those hurt by abortion. From 2007–2010, I spoke and wrote about recovery from abortion with Ruth Graham & Friends conferences. In 2012, my book *Cradle My Heart: Finding God's Love After Abortion* was published, pointing women to the healing and freedom we find in Jesus Christ. Currently, I host a weekly live and interactive radio program inviting discussion with everyday people and experts in faith to help on the healing journey. I have even let go of my stage name that kept me bound to my former sinful self-reliance and fear. I'm finally free. Truly, God makes everything beautiful in His time (Ecclesiastes 3:11).

If you would like to know more about Kim's story and ministry, you may visit her website at www.KimKetola.com.

Your Own Worst Enemy

You may feel as if you've done something so awful that God could not possibly forgive you. You may think you are unredeemable or that your circumstances are beyond hope. However, the Bible says otherwise. Even though God freely offers forgiveness, we often refuse to accept it. Psalm 32:5 says, "I acknowledged my sin to you, and I did not cover my iniquity; I said, 'I will confess my transgressions to the LORD,' and you forgave the iniquity of my sin." Once you confess your sins, the guilt is forgiven. Resting in this truth can allow the load of guilt you are feeling to be lifted and cast into the depths of the sea, never to be remembered by God again (Psalm 103:12).

Perhaps you are in a difficult trial through no fault of your own. One day you will see what God is doing through your suffering. Trials are not wasted time. They are opportunities to experience the growth and change we need. God is using them to change and mold us into the likeness of Christ.

Suffering with the Right Attitude

The Old Testament tells the story of a man named Job, who was one of the wealthiest men of his day. He was blessed with a large family, a huge staff of servants, and untold wealth in livestock. He also had friends who honored and respected him. He was a man of integrity and righteousness.

Job's seven sons and three daughters enjoyed lives of plenty. Job wanted them to know God, serve God, and live upright lives.

Not only did Job have the respect of men, but God was pleased with him as well. Job 1:8 and 2:3 record God's estimation of Job: "And the LORD said to Satan, 'Have you considered my servant Job, that there is none like him on the earth, a blameless and upright man, who fears God and turns away from evil?'" Can you imagine God boasting about you that way?

Satan, however, disputed God's appraisal of this "blameless" man. "Why wouldn't Job love You when You've given him every-thing his heart desires?" he challenged. "What would happen if all of his blessings were taken away?" Many of us would fail such a test, but God knew Job's heart.

Satan asked God to allow him to disrupt Job's life to see what he was really made of. God agreed, but He set boundaries regarding what Satan could do. Everything Job had could be taken, but Job himself could not be touched.

The enemy eagerly began destroying Job's life. Raiders stole all of his oxen, donkeys, and camels and killed all but one of his field workers. Fire destroyed all of Job's sheep and killed all but one of his shepherds. Then a whirlwind destroyed Job's house and killed all of his children.

For Job, the loss of his wealth was upsetting enough, but the loss of his children devastated him. If they were in his position, many people would have become angry toward God. Yet Job chose to continue serving Him.

Job knew that everything he had was from God. Therefore, God had the authority to take it all away. In the midst of his loss, Job said, "'Naked I came from my mother's womb, and naked shall I return. The LORD gave, and the LORD has taken away; blessed be the name of the LORD.' In all this Job did not sin or charge God with wrong" (Job 1:21–22).

Despite his loss, Job did not sin by telling God that He was wrong for allowing him to experience all of this suffering. Such loyalty was possible because of Job's longstanding and intimate relationship with God. We can only imagine that as he worked his way "up the corporate ladder," Job had seen that others who had worked just as hard were not enjoying the same kind of success. Instead of becoming proud, he humbled himself. Job thanked God for His blessings and used his wealth to help others. It was only because of this experience that he could say from his heart, "The LORD gave and the LORD has taken away." The process of humbly walking with God through the good times prepared him to do the same in the bad times.

Satan was not ready to give up. When God once again presented Job as a model of righteousness, Satan argued that Job only worshipped Him because he still had his health. Satan asked God to allow him to strike Job's body with a serious illness. Satan was convinced that no one could pass that test, not even Job. So God gave Satan license to strike Job with painful physical ailments under the condition that Job's life be spared. Even when Satan attacked Job, he could not cross the boundaries God had set. God was still in control.

Job's body became covered with sores, from the soles of his feet to the crown of his head. The sores must have itched and oozed because the Bible says that Job sat in ashes and scraped the sores with pottery shards. Sitting or lying down for any length of time must have been horrendously painful. In spite of his misery, the Bible says that Job continued to trust his Heavenly Father. When his wife advised him to "curse God and die" (Job 2:9), Job refused to do so. He chose to accept whatever God allowed into his life.

When Job's friends heard about his suffering, three of them came to visit him. For a week, Eliphaz, Bildad, and Zophar sat quietly with Job, saying nothing. Then they broke their silence by pronouncing their assessment of the situation. They told him that all of these hardships must have come upon him because he had sinned in some way. They believed he must have been cursed for some evil he had committed.

When Job realized he was not going to get any compassion or encouragement from his wife or friends, he felt as if life was not worth living. He wailed, "Why did I not die at birth, come out from the womb and expire?" (Job 3:11). But the Lord reminded Job that He is God, and those He created have no right to make demands. God asked, "Where were you when I laid the foundation of the earth? Tell me, if you have understanding. Who determined its measurements—surely you know! Or who stretched the line upon it?" (Job 38:4–5). God continued this string of rhetorical questions. He asked, "Where were you when I caused the stars to sing? Can you command the dawn and cause it to break forth? Where is the dwelling place of light and darkness? Can you determine when the animals of the earth give birth? Can you give a horse strength? Tell me, if you know these things!" (Job 38–39).

Job listened to all the Lord had to say and repented of his despondence. When he bowed his heart again to God, he was comforted. God then restored Job's health and his fortunes. He became even wealthier than before. God also blessed him with many more sons and daughters. In the end, Job's friends, who thought they had his situation all figured out, were proven wrong. They learned of God's character, steadfastness, and sovereignty.

We know there was no hidden sin in Job because we are given the backstory. Few of us, however, rise to that level of righteousness. If sin is nagging at your conscience, you may feel as if God is giving you the punishment you deserve. Although such a reaction is human, that isn't the way God works. Because He loves us, He sometimes disciplines us to bring sin to our attention and to restore our intimate fellowship with Him. Other times, He allows suffering even when we haven't sinned for the reward of growing closer to Him.

Attitude of Gratitude

The book of Job gives us insight into God's desire for humility and submission, but the book of James tells us that God wants more. He actually wants us to rejoice in suffering! We are told, "Count it all joy, my brothers, when you meet trials of various kinds, for you know that the testing of your faith produces steadfastness. And let steadfastness have its full effect, that you may be perfect and complete, lacking in nothing" (James 1:2–4).

It is challenging enough not to complain about life's trials, but God actually wants us to be joyful in the midst of them. How is that possible? The answer lies in considering the fruit that your trials will ultimately produce. Being tested develops perseverance, increases our trust in God, and deepens our relationship with Him. Focusing on this truth can help us respond to trials with attitudes that please God.

Job's faith was strengthened and purified through his trial. His love and respect for God was independent of his circumstances. He trusted that whatever suffering God allowed would be worth it in the end.

Pain can turn a person into a monster who lashes out or a minister who empathizes. God told Job to pray that his friends wouldn't be cursed for their arrogance. I think God commanded that to help keep Job's heart pure in the context of their emotional callousness. More importantly, we can imagine that for the rest of his life, Job was more understanding of others who suffered and was better able to minister to them.

You can be a blessing to those around you too. Pray for others, even those who are in the wrong, and God will do amazing things. You don't have to defend yourself or prove that you are right. Let God take up your case.

God's plan is ultimately for the benefit of His kingdom. Whatever hardships you are experiencing right now can be used to glorify Him. He doesn't always tell us what He's doing, but we need to trust Him anyway. Obedience and the right attitude close the gaps in our spiritual armor so that Satan has no opportunity to gain entry.

No matter how painful your situation, it's not about your discomfort. It's about giving God the glory He is due and experiencing the growth and fellowship with Him that He wants to produce in you.

Angry at God

Have you ever been angry at God because of the painful things you've endured? You might be reluctant to admit it because you think it's a sin to be mad at God. Besides, since God is perfect and never does anything wrong, how could you be mad at Him?

A counselor once asked me if I was angry at God for some of the things that had happened to me. I replied, "I'm not angry at God.

I'm upset with my situation." My counselor said, "If you are angry at your circumstances, which God allowed, that means you're mad at God." I'd never thought about it like that before, but I finally made the connection. As much as I hated to admit it, I had to repent of being angry at God and acknowledge that my anger was hindering my fellowship with Him.

How do you know if you are angry toward God? First, are you praying and reading the Bible regularly? Is your attitude preventing you from spending time with God? Do you feel cynical and untrusting? When someone else succeeds or reaches a place in life you wish to be, do you feel jealous of that person or anxious about your own situation?

We all have occasions when we are tempted to become angry at God for not allowing our circumstances to be different. The solution is to recognize our attitudes and allow God to correct them before we stop trusting Him and start shutting Him out of our lives. Even when you don't feel like it, I encourage you to spend time reading the Bible and dwelling on God's promises, especially those that pertain to your situation. Pray for God to give you confidence and the peace you need to respond to those around you in love. Choose to believe that God loves you and has great plans for you. As He says in His Word: "The LORD is faithful in all his words and kind in all his works" (Psalm 145:13).

God already knows how you feel, so don't be afraid to be honest. Tell Him where you are struggling to trust Him. Confess any bitterness or lack of faith. God will hear your prayer and restore your heart to the right place.

When Others Are Suffering

When something goes wrong in someone else's life, don't try to cast blame or criticize them as Job's friends did. Instead, strive for gentleness, understanding, and wisdom. Seeking the wisdom of

God will protect you from arrogance and give you discernment in every situation.

If you think someone is suffering because of a bad attitude or poor decision, humbly consider your own failures. Remember the "plank-eye principle" from Matthew 7:1–5. Ask questions about their experience rather than rushing to condemn them. Give the person the freedom to speak to you, then listen to what he or she tells you. James 1:19 says, "Know this, my beloved brothers: let every person be quick to hear, slow to speak, slow to anger." Your goal in helping others through trials should be to bring them closer to Christ.

The character we portray will either draw people to God's truth or push them away from it. We can share God's Word with our mouths, but it's important that we live it out as well. Forcing our views upon others will not bear good fruit. We must exhibit sincerity with a gentle spirit for our words to ring true. In both word and deed, we are to exercise wisdom.

If Job's friends had demonstrated those qualities, they would have been a comfort to Job instead of a source of additional pain. One thing those men did do right, however, was to spend time with Job and grieve with him. Sometimes just being there for someone is the most meaningful and beneficial action you can take.

Attitude Is a Choice

Some people claim they can't change their attitudes toward suffering because they feel helpless against their emotions. They say, "I can't change how I feel." It's true that our emotions—our initial reactions to an event—are not under our direct control. In themselves, emotions are neither good nor bad. During a trial you might feel hurt, angry, frustrated, or sad. That's okay. However, in contrast to our emotions is our attitude. In other words, you can't help how you feel, but what you do with those feelings is up to you.

Some people respond to suffering by shutting down emotionally and becoming depressed. If you become tempted to do that, reflecting more on the Lord and less on yourself will enable God to take His rightful place at the center of your life. Sometimes, right actions can help us develop right attitudes. Jesus says, "You have heard that it was said, 'You shall love your neighbor and hate your enemy.' But I say to you, Love your enemies and pray for those who persecute you" (Matthew 5:43–44). Praying for our enemies and doing good to them can transform anger and hatred into love.

Jesus is our primary example of a right attitude toward suffering. "For to this you have been called, because Christ also suffered for you, leaving you an example, so that you might follow in his steps. He committed no sin, neither was deceit found in his mouth. When he was reviled, he did not revile in return; when he suffered, he did not threaten, but continued entrusting himself to him who judges justly" (1 Peter 2:21–23).

The key to Jesus' obedience and submission was trust. Whatever occurred in Jesus' life, He remained rooted in His relationship with the Father. He had cultivated that trust through the choice to spend time with God, learn His Word, and obey Him throughout His life. We, too, can grow in our trust relationship with God so that when trials come, we remain confident of His goodness and love.

Scott's Story

The following testimony demonstrates how our attitudes affect our ability to be used by God. If we remain open to whatever God wants to do in us, having a positive attitude can help us through the toughest struggles. If we don't, we will most likely be defeated. Scott's story shows that keeping our hearts and minds directed toward Christ makes all the difference.

∽

On April 19, 1995, 168 people lost their lives when the Alfred P. Murrah Federal Building in Oklahoma City was bombed. Two years later, I took seventy-five high school students on a mission trip to work in the city's surrounding communities, which were still recovering from the attack. Little did I know that God led me to Oklahoma City to teach me a bigger lesson about who He really is and how much He loves me.

At that time, I was serving as a student pastor in a small town in northeast Mississippi. By human standards, my ministry was a success. We were busy. Students and adults were faithfully giving their time for the sake of the gospel. We were not prideful or arrogant. We were just working hard and praying that our efforts would please the Lord. If you had asked me during those days if I thought the Lord was happy with my work, I would have said, "Absolutely." I was confident that I was fulfilling God's plan.

During the week in Oklahoma, our schedule was full. In the daytime, we ministered to children who lived on the outskirts of the city. At night, we held what I refer to as old-time revival services in a Native American church. At the end of each day, I hosted a debrief time with my students and other volunteers, talking about what the Lord was doing and going over what we had planned for the next day.

By the second day, my students were already growing tired and bickering with one another. That night, I attempted to refocus their attention on the purpose of our trip, but I felt so physically drained that my legs barely held me up. When I took my seat on the bus to return to our hotel, I wrote in my Bible, "Mission Tour 1997—God is getting ready to do something miraculous."

When I got to my room around 10 p.m., I called my wife in Mississippi and asked her to lift me up in prayer because I did not feel well. I asked her to pray that God would not allow me to be taken out of service for the rest of the trip. I had no idea where God would lead my wife and me over the next few days.

As soon as I hung up the phone, I slipped into a neurological coma that lasted seven days. Two well-intentioned adults drove me back home to Mississippi rather than taking me to a local emergency room. They called my wife and suggested she meet us at the hospital in Columbus.

When we arrived at the hospital, I was admitted to the intensive care unit. After running an extensive battery of tests, the doctors discovered that I had contracted viral encephalitis, a deadly disease that attacks the brain. Three-and-a-half days into my coma, the doctors told my family I probably wouldn't make it through the night. While my wife underwent the most challenging moment of her life, I experienced the peace of God that surpasses all understanding (Philippians 4:7). As I lay comatose, God had my undivided attention.

Unbeknownst to me at the time, a pastor whom I had never met (but who lived in the same city I did) arrived home after preaching on Sunday morning and heard God tell him to go to the hospital: "I have someone for you to see there." God told him to get dressed in his "church clothes," which for him meant his black suit and white priest's collar. As he started toward the door, the Lord said, "Take your oil. I have someone for you to anoint and pray over."

At the hospital, he visited a sick church member but knew that wasn't all God had planned. He turned to leave, not sure where else to go. Just then a nurse asked if he would visit a neurological patient whose family had just been called in to say their final goodbyes.

The pastor walked into my ICU room and told the nurse, "I'm here to see Reverend Scott Hall." The instant my name was spoken, I awoke from the coma and sat up in bed. The pastor took my hand and preached from the book of Joel. In a fiery tone he said, "You will walk and talk again. You will do ministry in the name of our Lord again. God told me to tell you that this disease is not because of sin in your life but to reveal Himself to you." He anointed my head with oil and prayed over me. When he turned to leave the room, I fell back into the coma and remained unconscious for three-and-a-half more days.

My family was overjoyed by what they saw. God had answered their prayers! But later that afternoon, their faith was shaken when my condition deteriorated. That evening, six neurological specialists came in from the University of Alabama Medical Center and had me flown to Birmingham, where they would oversee my medical care.

On July 23, 1997, I was moved from the ICU to a private room. I regained consciousness, but no one else was aware of it. I could see and hear those who entered my room, but I couldn't talk, walk, or even move my hands. I had no memory of what had happened to me. The only thing I remembered was being visited by God's messenger, who had reassured me that I would walk, talk, and minister again.

God told me two things as I lay there. First, He said, "Scott, I love you." God had stripped me of everything so I could understand that He loves me in a way that has nothing to do with my performance. Next, He said, "Scott, I want you to love others with this same kind of love." God was talking about love with no strings attached.

When I finally became responsive, I felt incredible peace about my recovery and my mission. I had a renewed sense of purpose and was eager to follow my new call. Both my immediate family and my church family provided great support during that time. As I turned the corner and began to recover, I went into rehab, and my family's support became all the more precious to me. To this day, I treasure the moments we shared.

I looked with new eyes on the youth I served in my ministry. Suddenly I saw them as God sees them, which transformed the way I related to them. Things that had previously irritated me meant nothing compared to how much I loved them. I wanted nothing more than to share God's incredible love and His amazing plans for their lives so they would be encouraged to live out their faith in the world.

Because God sacrificed His precious Son out of love for me, I need to give my life as a sacrifice for others. I want to be poured out as a blessing (Philippians 2:17). For the past fifteen years, I have lived in the blessed assurance of God's love for me. Now my only goal is to love the Lord my God with all my heart, soul, and mind, and to love my neighbor as myself (Matthew 22:37–40).

I would never have asked to be put into a coma, but God used it to renew me. For that, I will be eternally grateful.

Scott's situation could have led to despair and anger, but he kept his focus on God and stayed open to how God wanted to use his experience. Because of that attitude, God was able to let Scott know how much He loved him and show him His purpose: to love others.

We can trust God in all of our trials and know that He will somehow use them to transform us and, perhaps, many others. We will shine on the other side of our trials if we don't give up or give in to bitterness. God is not insensitive to our suffering. He is sufficient for all our needs. He wants us to hold on to Him and be careful not to judge others who are suffering.

In John 9:1–3 it says, "As he passed by, he saw a man blind from birth. And his disciples asked him, 'Rabbi, who sinned, this man or his parents, that he was born blind?' Jesus answered, 'It was not that this man sinned, or his parents, but that the works of God might be displayed in him.'" In the same way, God uses your hardships to fulfill His purposes in and through your life.

Perhaps what you are experiencing has the potential to minister to someone in a meaningful way. Pray that God would open your spiritual eyes to the opportunities you have to share His love and faithfulness.

For Such a Time as This

One of the most amazing stories about the value of perseverance is found in the book of Esther in the Old Testament.

Esther was a young Jewish woman of unusual beauty whose people were exiles in the ancient country of Persia. After Esther's parents died, her cousin Mordecai brought her into his family and raised her as his own daughter. In a nationwide beauty contest, Xerxes, king of Persia, chose Esther as his queen. She transitioned into a new life in a palace where the furniture was made of gold and silver, the gardens were lush, and the wine was unlimited. The king liked Esther so much that he threw a banquet in her honor and assigned attendants to meet her every need.

Esther's life of comfort became threatened when Mordecai reported to her that Haman, a royal official, planned to annihilate every Jewish person in all 127 provinces under Xerxes' rule. Haman had been offended that Mordecai, because of his beliefs as a Jew, would not bow down to him. He was so angry that he wanted to kill every Jew in the kingdom. Haman obtained the king's blessing to carry out his evil plan. Mordecai asked Esther to intercede with Xerxes to prevent this genocide.

Esther wasn't sure whether she could persuade Xerxes to change the decree, but time was of the essence. If she waited until she was summoned to make her plea, it might be too late to save her people. But it was against the law to appear before the king without a summons. If she did, she could be killed immediately.

Mordecai understood that God appoints people for particular tasks at certain times, and he suspected that God had placed Esther into a royal position for just this reason. He urged her, "For if you keep silent at this time, relief and deliverance will rise for the Jews from another place, but you and your father's house will perish. And who knows whether you have not come to the kingdom for such a time as this?" (Esther 4:14).

Esther may have thought about the many benefits she enjoyed at the palace. She could have basked in her own glory, thinking, *I am so beautiful and such a special person. I deserve all of this.* She could have reasoned, *I feel sorry for my people, but I don't have to get involved in this. Things might be better for me if I keep my identity a secret.*

If Esther had thought this way, God would still have intervened, but her story would have turned out very differently. However, Esther realized that she had become queen not just for her own benefit, but also for the benefit of others. She told Mordecai, "Go, gather all the Jews to be found in Susa, and hold a fast on my behalf, and do not eat or drink for three days, night or day. I and my young women will also fast as you do. Then I will go to the king, though it is against the law, and if I perish, I perish" (Esther 4:16).

Esther was committed to doing the right thing. She put aside any concern about her life and well-being. She determined to do what she could to save her people by approaching the king, and then she left the results in God's hands.

Esther invited the king to two banquets. At the second, she did what no one in the kingdom was allowed to do. She approached the king uninvited. At great risk to her life, she revealed her identity as a Jew and pleaded with the king to repeal the verdict dictating death for the Jewish people. The king had every right to put Esther to death, but out of his love for her, he spared her.

King Xerxes could not rescind the original decree to attack the Jews, but he issued a new law that gave Jews the authority to defend themselves from those who tried to harm them. In the end, the enemies of the Jews were defeated and Haman was hung in the public square. Xerxes decreed that the Jews could establish the holiday of Purim. Mordecai, Esther's cousin, was elevated to second in command in the kingdom.

Will You Be an Esther?

While our stories might not be as dramatic as Esther's, God has nonetheless called us to fulfill our destinies. Though lives may not hang in the immediate balance of our decisions, eternal souls do. God has called us to unique roles in His kingdom, and we may have to experience significant adversity to perform them. Your risk might not be possible death, but God's call will often take you out of your comfort zone. You can face the risk, run from it, or simply ignore it.

A man named James worked in an office with both believers and unbelievers. For weeks, God put a coworker named Tim on his mind. James seemed to run into Tim often—in the elevator, on break, and even outside of work. They greeted each other politely, but James knew that God wanted him to pray for Tim and spend time with him. James decided to ask his coworker to lunch, get to know him better, and hopefully share the gospel with him. Despite this commitment, James found his schedule busy with work and personal plans. *I'll ask him to lunch sometime soon,* he thought.

One day when James went to work, he learned that Tim had quit unexpectedly. His boss said that Tim's father was terminally ill, and Tim had decided it would be best to move back to his hometown immediately. James regretted that he had failed to take advantage of the opportunity to reach out to Tim. He wished he had followed the promptings God placed on his heart in a timely manner.

Is there something God has called you to do—a specific task that He has repeatedly laid in front of you—but you keep putting it off? God could choose to fulfill His purposes through someone else, but He has asked you. Will you go on the adventure of obeying God's call? Even if trial and suffering are involved, God is greater than any danger you might face. He can make every event reflect His glory and cause each circumstance to turn out for the good of His people.

A Father's Love

Risking loss to do something important goes against our natural tendencies. Be honest with the Lord. Confess your fears and short-comings, and ask God for His strength. Take comfort in knowing that God's loving-kindness is everlasting and that His tender mercies toward you never fail. Jeremiah 31:3 says, "I have loved you with an everlasting love; therefore I have continued my faithfulness to you."

Think about the love a good father has for his children. No matter how secure the father's children feel in that love, they will often kick against his will, shouting things like, "That's not fair! You don't want me to have any fun!" As children mature and become wise, they begin to understand and appreciate their father's wisdom. Likewise, when we open our hearts to God, we make room for Him to work not only in our circumstances, but in our hearts. We allow God to weed out the sin and bad attitudes that hinder our walks with Him. Once God has filtered out the impurities, we see Him with new eyes and are able to grasp—perhaps for the first time—how much He loves us and cares about the details of our lives.

Seasons in Life

When we feel like giving up, we can take comfort in knowing that whatever we are experiencing is just for a season. We find a beautiful reminder of this truth in Ecclesiastes 3:1–8, which says,

> For everything there is a season, and a time for every matter under heaven: a time to be born, and a time to die; a time to plant, and a time to pluck up what is planted; a time to kill, and a time to heal; a time to break down, and a time to build up; a time to weep, and a time to laugh; a time to mourn, and a time to dance; a time to cast away stones, and a time to gather stones together; a time to embrace, and a time to refrain from embracing; a time to seek, and a time to lose; a time to keep, and a time to cast away; a time to tear, and a time to sew; a time to keep silence, and a time to speak; a time to love, and a time to hate; a time for war, and a time for peace.

Seasons in our lives may be as varied as the physical seasons of the year, but Jesus is Lord of them all. If you are in a place you would not have chosen, trust that God's purpose, whatever it is, will be accomplished. Like Esther, you are being used by God in the time and place you are in right now.

Marie sat in the hospital, waiting for her husband of forty-five years to awaken after surgery on his cheek. His cancer had returned and the surgeons had performed skin grafts. Tubes protruded from every orifice. There was a breathing tube in his throat. Their two grandsons, ages thirteen and ten, came to be with them in the hospital. At lunchtime, Marie took them to the cafeteria. While they were eating, the boys asked questions about God, wanting to know why He allowed this to happen to their grandfather. Marie talked about the great love God had for them and gave examples of how He had been caring for them throughout this difficult season. Over lunch, each of the boys made a decision to receive

Jesus' free gift of eternal life. As trying as the situation was, God provided a beautiful opportunity that changed the lives and eternal destinies of Marie's grandsons.

The Apostle James writes, "Blessed is the man who remains steadfast under trial, for when he has stood the test he will receive the crown of life, which God has promised to those who love him" (James 1:12). Every time we come through a challenge, we are changed. Each new victory makes us stronger in faith and more able to praise God for His faithfulness. Through our struggles, we come to understand the heart and character of God in a way that we otherwise would not.

Just as a butterfly cannot survive unless it breaks through a tough cocoon, we need adversity to make our spiritual muscles strong. If someone were to assist the butterfly in emerging from its cocoon, it would die soon afterward because its wings would be too weak to fly. Sometimes our Heavenly Father helps us quickly break free of our trials. Other times He allows us to remain in our struggles—to see them through—in order to "strengthen our wings" so the next time a problem comes along we are able to soar above it. In the midst of our suffering, we must do whatever God calls us to do.

Cheryl's Story

When I think of the ability to soar above circumstances, I think of Cheryl. While experiencing tremendous disappointment, Cheryl chose to trust God's plan for her. Because she was obedient in the extremely difficult situation in which God placed her, He used her to accomplish His will.

$\backsim$

My journey began at the age of twenty-five when I received Jesus Christ as my personal Savior. Raymond, to whom I had been married six years at the time, saw that I had changed from the woman he'd originally married. He wanted nothing to do with Jesus. While my heart ached for my husband's salvation, God answered my prayers for the salvation of my daughters: Zena, age five, and Tasha, age four.

Thus began the process of God conforming me into the image of Jesus Christ. Though my husband wasn't a believer, the Lord used the situation to bring me to maturity. My obligation was simply to do the right thing. The rest was in God's hands.

When I accepted Christ, the concept of submission was foreign to me. Because I loved Jesus and wanted to please Him, I knew He would help me. I could only submit by the supernatural power of the Holy Spirit. I'll admit, it wasn't easy. Submission is a work of the heart. Proverbs 23:26 reads, "My son [or daughter], give me your heart, and let your eyes observe my ways." God can heal a broken heart, but only if we give Him all the pieces.

Raymond and I were married for thirty-two years. God used those years of his unbelief to teach me the depth of love found only in Jesus Christ while breaking, melting, molding, and filling me, then allowing me to be used for His glory. In Philippians 1:6, Paul wrote, "And I am sure of this, that he who began a good work in you will bring it to completion at the day of Jesus Christ."

Because I was thirsty for more of God, I got into the Word and faithfully attended church, not only for Sunday worship but also for midweek Bible studies and prayer meetings. Before long, my husband insisted that I attend only on Sunday mornings. I was upset, but I agreed, knowing that just as Christ had learned obedience through suffering, the Holy Spirit was teaching me a new way to connect with God. The Bible says, "For God is not unjust so as to overlook your work and the love that you have shown for his name in serving the saints, as you still do" (Hebrews 6:10).

I was a Sunday-morning-only Christian for a year, and during that season, the Holy Spirit showed me that my spiritual growth wasn't dependent on church attendance. He showed me that it was dependent on my personal time alone with the Lord. I purchased a commentary, a Bible dictionary, and other study tools. By the end of that year, the Lord dealt with my husband's heart, and he allowed me to resume attending church any time I desired to do so.

What the enemy meant for evil, God meant for good. We read in Proverbs 21:1, "The king's heart is a stream of water in the hand of the LORD; he turns it wherever he will." That time of waiting on the Lord prepared me to be what I am today: a women's Bible teacher with a burden to share the wisdom and knowledge of Christ.

As days turned into months and then years, I wondered why Raymond had not come to the Lord. After being a faithful follower of Christ for sixteen years, I felt God was obligated to save my husband. I grew angry because many of my friends' husbands were coming to salvation, but mine had not. Then my pastor reassured me that God was in control and that His timing would be perfect. My responsibility was to remain faithful.

When I hit the big "40" in 1987, I was frustrated. Our nest was empty, but our marriage was not what I thought it should be. My husband and I didn't seem to really know each other anymore, and we had become more like roommates than a married couple. I cried for six months before the Lord showed me the hole in my heart and opened my eyes to the truth that my satisfaction could only be found in Jesus Christ. The gulf between my husband and me was growing wider, but that reality only provoked me to pray harder and praise God even more.

On February 10, 2004, Raymond had a massive stroke. A few days later, after our pastor witnessed to him, I took Raymond's hand and asked him if he had received Jesus Christ as his personal Savior. He squeezed my hand several times to confirm that he had. On February 17, 2004, God took him home to heaven. In seven days, God accomplished what had taken thirty-two years of preparation!

It comforts me to know that God's ways are perfect and everything that happens is part of His plan. I am now on the other side of His grace, and I embrace the plans He has for me, plans for a future and a hope. It was a blessing to have been able to encourage and teach women about the joy of living above their circumstances at the Ruth Graham & Friends conferences from 2008–2009.

Can you imagine being married to an unbeliever for thirty-two years and trying to hold on to hope while waiting for God to move? Cheryl submitted to her husband's authority out of a heart of obedience to Christ. Even when she did not understand, she continued to trust that God would reach her husband. In the flesh, such patience and obedience would be impossible. But when we press into God and choose to believe that His way is best, we can rest in faith and be at peace no matter how long the wait.

Cheryl did not attempt to force her husband to change. Neither should we try to force others to change in the middle of our struggles so things will be easier on us. We must obey God in faith, especially when obedience is difficult. If we are to live in faith (as we so often say we do), we must choose to trust God, believing that He is producing in us the peaceful fruit of righteousness. Only by trusting Him can we more closely resemble Jesus. Once we begin to look at things in that light, we can know that the end of the story will be good.

God may choose to let us see resolutions in this life, but sometimes He may not. Whatever the outcome of our situations, we know that glorifying Him is the ultimate goal. We must obey whatever the cost, leaving the results in God's hands. If we pray and live to serve Him, we will have no regrets. We will know that He will accomplish His purposes whether we understand them or not.

Redefining Victory

*T*hese days, many people have a Global Positioning System (GPS) in their vehicles or on their cell phones. Once it is programmed, a helpful little voice tells them which direction to travel, where to turn, and when they've arrived at their destination. I have a Garmin GPS, but I must confess, I'm a bit stubborn. Sometimes I don't listen to my device because I think I know a better way to go. When I venture out on my own, my Garmin persistently repeats, "Recalculating . . . Recalculating . . ." Much to my chagrin, I frequently find that Garmin really does know the best way, or at least a quicker one.

Christians have an internal GPS too—God's Perfect Son. If we listen to His voice through the Holy Spirit, He will guide our every step. He tells us what pitfalls to avoid and safely gets us where we need to go. Isaiah 30:21 says, "And your ears shall hear a word behind you, saying, 'This is the way, walk in it,' when you turn to the right or when you turn to the left." God sometimes recalculates my course too, usually because I've made a wrong turn somewhere along the way. Fortunately, I can always count on His perfect knowledge of the route and His ability to get me back on track.

In the journey of life, the best route is not always the fastest or the easiest. The next time you see others receive blessing upon blessing while you work two jobs just to make ends meet, resist the urge to be envious. God's plan for you is as special as His plan is for them. Your plan is custom-made for you.

There have been times when I have been jealous of other people's lives. I have watched a lot of my friends get married, have children, and live lives that I admired while I have remained single. Growing up, I had learning disabilities and felt as if everyone else was smarter than I was. Trials seemed to surround me, while others appeared to live problem free and radiate a joy I didn't have. I thought I would be happier if my circumstances were different. Although I knew other people faced their own pain and heartache, I thought if I could deal with fewer problems, I would experience victory. I learned that my problems weren't based on my circumstances; they were based on my lack of trust in God's custom-made plan for my life. His plan was—and is—much better than mine. I think I know what's best for me, but I don't see the big picture the way God does. I only see bits and pieces. When I confessed my lack of trust in God, I began to experience His peace, even though my situation remained the same.

Perhaps the best thing to do when you are frustrated with your circumstances is to release the expectations you have for your life. Discontentment comes when we believe that we *should* be making more money, *should* be married or single, *should* have accomplished certain things, and so on. If your current reality differs from your expectations, admit to God that you are not satisfied. Ask Him to help you be content. Let Him walk with you in reaching for your goals. Be open to the possibility that He may direct you to change them.

What Is True Victory?

How can we experience victory in the midst of pain? First, let's take a look at what true victory really is.

Many people believe they will have victory once a storm has passed or a painful season ends, but that's not the definition of victory. More often than not, victory doesn't require a change of circumstances; it requires a change in perspective. Under this definition, we can experience victory during each minute of the storm. When we choose to trust God rather than our point of view, we experience His peace. That kind of peace brings triumph over the trial even before it ends. If we hold on to our faith even while the storm is raging, we will experience true victory. When we are trusting God, we are experiencing His victory regardless of our circumstances.

We usually view our circumstances through the filter of what we know or our past experiences. For instance, when a tree falls, a botanist might examine the age of the tree and its health, a logger might look at the quality and usefulness of the wood, and a real estate agent might determine the effect of the tree's absence on the value of a property. Just as different people view the same situation in various ways, God's perspective is vastly different from ours. We must trust His goodness in all our circumstances. Job 37:5 says, "God thunders wondrously with his voice; he does great things that we cannot comprehend."

Our ability to redefine victory is refined throughout the lifelong process of knowing God. Knowing Him more intimately will change our character to reflect Him more clearly. It is impossible to know God completely, but we will continue to gain a deeper understanding if we draw near to Him in worship and spend time in His presence. God will reveal glimpses of Himself to those who set aside their own agendas and ask Him to reveal His heart to them, even when they can't see the full picture.

How can you begin to see a bigger picture? Start by changing the questions you ask. "Why is this happening, God?" reveals a focus on your will rather than God's. Your plans are not as important as God's (and certainly are less grand). Instead ask, "What do You want to do in me—or through me—in the midst of this?" This question seeks God's perspective on the situation.

Isaiah contrasts these two perspectives when he says, "For my thoughts are not your thoughts, neither are your ways my ways, declares the LORD. For as the heavens are higher than the earth, so are my ways higher than your ways and my thoughts than your thoughts" (Isaiah 55:8–9). Victory is not just arriving at the destination God has set for us. Victory is trusting Him each minute of the journey. The point of the journey is not the destination, but your relationship with the eternal GPS.

Kingdom Power

Sometimes God's ways just don't make sense to us. This is as true today as it was in the days of Jesus. The Bible contains some wonderful examples of people called by God to do things that didn't make sense to others.

When Paul and Barnabas started preaching to the crowds in Antioch, the people looked on their message favorably. A week later, the people had a very different reaction: "The next Sabbath almost the whole city gathered to hear the word of the Lord. But when the Jews saw the crowds, they were filled with jealousy and began to contradict what was spoken by Paul, reviling him" (Acts 13:44–45).

Paul and Barnabas could have questioned why God would lead them to be among such people, but they responded in a way that honored God. They didn't yield to the Jews' cruelty by being unkind in return or running away to save their own lives. Instead, they courageously obeyed God in sharing the gospel in the synagogue. They weren't shaken because they knew God had a plan to extend His kingdom. Scripture says, "And Paul and Barnabas spoke out boldly, saying, 'It was necessary that the word of God be spoken first to you. Since you thrust it aside and judge yourselves unworthy of eternal life, behold, we are turning to the Gentiles'" (Acts 13:46). Sharing the Word of God with the Gentiles was unheard of at that time, but to Paul and Barnabas, their calling was clear.

They recognized that, through their rejection by their fellow Jews in Antioch, God was pointing them toward a new ministry.

King David was the second king of Israel and the author of many of the Psalms. Before taking the throne, David was a mighty warrior favored by Saul, Israel's first king. Over time, Saul became deeply envious of David's triumphs in battle and sought to kill him.

King Saul repeatedly disobeyed God. For example, in 1 Samuel 15, God told Saul to destroy everything from the battle with the Amalekites, yet the king kept some of the spoils. Saul also disobeyed by performing a burnt offering, a role reserved only for the priests. He did things his own way—not God's—which caused God to remove him from the throne.

Although David knew that God had prepared him for kingship and that he would eventually be crowned, this mighty man of God didn't attempt to take the throne by force. He did not even fight against Saul when Saul tried to kill him. Instead, he retreated to the desert and entrusted himself to God. As King Saul searched high and low, David hid out in the desert caves and waited on God's sovereign timing. David trusted the Lord through his suffering.

One night, David found Saul sound asleep in one of the caves. As he looked down at the king, David could have easily rationalized, *If I kill Saul, I can end all of this turmoil. This is the perfect chance to destroy my enemy and get past this persecution—it is a true gift from God!* However, rather than commit murder, David cut off a piece of Saul's robe and left, vowing that he would never harm the one God had anointed (1 Samuel 24:5-7). If there were any revenge to be taken, David would trust God with it. In the end, King Saul was killed in battle and David took his rightful place on the throne. God was the one who judged Saul, not David.

It is easy to use human logic when dealing with trials. Fleshly reactions and sin can cloud our discernment. But when we try to force our way and rationalize our behavior, we are not relying on

God. If David had killed Saul, he would have been relying on his own strength and overstepped the boundaries God had placed around him. If he had cut short God's time of waiting, he would have been ultimately dissatisfied. David knew that if God had chosen him to be king, God Himself would usher him to the throne.

God wants us to humble our hearts and come to Him like trusting children (Matthew 18:3–4). When we do, He gives us wisdom, works everything out for good, and blesses us because we please Him. In the middle of tough situations, God will comfort our hearts and give us peace as we obey Him.

Kristine's Story

Kristine experienced a parent's worst nightmare when her son died in a traffic accident. Yet in the midst of her grief, she felt the presence of God and trusted Him completely. Her testimony reminds us that God answers prayers, but He doesn't always answer them in the way we hope. God is gracious to reach out to us in love even when we can't comprehend the reason for our heartaches.

October 7, 2007, was a day much like any other. I picked up my son, Samuel, from high school and spent some time with him while he did his homework. Then we collected the other two children, Amanda and Joshua, from their home-school co-op classes, made a quick stop at Walmart, and headed home.

Of course, Sam wanted to drive. He'd gotten his license only months before and loved to get behind the wheel. He was a good driver, so I felt comfortable handing over the keys.

In fact, I looked forward to relaxing after spending the day chauffeuring the kids around.

The sun was setting early on that crisp autumn day. By the time we turned west onto the two-lane highway, the sun was blindingly low on the horizon. Then everything went black.

The next thing I remember was seeing the profile of a fireman peering through the shattered windshield of our 2000 Chevy Malibu. As I learned later, we had crossed the centerline and collided head on with a semi-truck. The car had spun multiple times until it landed on the side of the road. The powerful impact crushed our vehicle and pushed the hood to within inches of the front seat.

More emergency personnel arrived. As soon as we were freed from the vehicle with the Jaws of Life, Samuel was airlifted to Hennepin County Medical Center, a trauma center located forty miles away in downtown Minneapolis. Amanda, Josh, and I were driven to the local hospital by ambulance, and once our injuries were assessed, I was airlifted to HCMC. The children were transported there by ambulance.

Amanda was treated for a serious hematoma inside her spleen, several fractured ribs, and significant bruising on her abdomen from the seat belt. Josh broke his left tibia, right ankle, and left collarbone.

I was in serious condition, with a broken collarbone, left femur fracture, subarachnoid hematoma (bleeding in the head in the space that surrounds the brain), a partially collapsed lung, and a broken pelvis. My eyes crossed, and my blood pressure spiked. My leg was in traction in hopes of holding my pelvis together. I drifted in and out of consciousness, lost in a fog created by the combination of my head injury and the powerful pain medication.

My first memory in the hospital was of my friend Sandy walking into my room, a concerned look on her sweet face. All I knew at the time was that we'd been in a terrible accident.

"What's going on with Sam?" I asked. Somehow I knew Amanda and Josh were okay but that something was wrong with Sam.

Sandy knew she had to tell me the truth. "Sam hasn't woken up."

My son was in a coma with a brain-stem injury. He was in critical condition.

News of the accident spread quickly, and we received phone calls and emails from all over the United States, China, and Guatemala. Tens of thousands of people visited our Caring Bridge website to uplift and encourage the family. Buses full of people from churches and schools descended on the hospital. Around the clock there were between fifty and one hundred people praying for our family. It was an extraordinary outpouring of love.

After a couple of days, the hospital staff moved all four of us into one ICU room. My husband, Terry, moved from bed to bed, joining hands with us in love and prayer. His entire family could have been wiped out in an instant, yet his faith never faltered.

As the days passed, Sam's condition worsened. His temperature and heart rate soared and his muscles showed indications that they were failing. The prayers of our friends, family, and people we'd never even met intensified. Most people believed there was going to be healing for Sam, but one person was given a revelation that Sam was sitting with the

Father in heaven saying he didn't want to come back. I hoped for a miracle anyway.

On October 14, one week after the accident, the doctors determined that Sam no longer had any brain activity. It was time to see if he could breathe on his own.

As we gathered around his bedside, the nurse carefully unplugged the ventilator.

"Hey, Sam, it's time to wake up," I said, holding his hand.

There was no response. Sam's heartbeat and breathing both ceased. Our beautiful boy was gone. In anguish, we said our final goodbyes. Then I was rolled out of Sam's room in my hospital bed into a hallway filled with people. The next few days were a blur.

Sam's funeral took place on October 24, 2007, in his high school auditorium ten days after his passing. We'd had to delay the service so I would be strong enough to go. More than one thousand people attended the funeral.

After the burial, my life stopped. I'd not only lost my son, I'd also lost myself. The impact on my eyesight was significant, my hearing had declined dramatically, and my body, particularly my leg and hip, hurt constantly. I now experience crippling migraine headaches and epilepsy as a result of the brain injury. Every day, my physical challenges are reminders of the loss of my son.

There were times when I cried all day long. I'd put my head on my Bible, knowing that's where I needed to be, but I wasn't able to open it and hear what the Father had to say to me. I clung to the words from Jude 1:21: "Keep yourselves in the love of God, waiting for the mercy of our Lord Jesus Christ that leads to eternal life."

A few days after Sam died, my husband went to worship at our church. He was so sad, he couldn't even rise from his seat. All of a sudden, he had a vision of Sam running toward him through a field of gorgeous flowers. He said, "Dad, get up and bring as many people with you as you can. This is great!" Who could wish more for their son?

I know with absolute certainty that Sam is enjoying eternity in heaven because he had a personal relationship with Jesus. His favorite verse was 1 Corinthians 15:58: "Therefore, my beloved brothers, be steadfast, immovable, always abounding in the work of the Lord, knowing that in the Lord your labor is not in vain." That is how Sam lived his life. He loved to share his faith.

In one of his journal entries, Sam wrote that his biggest hope was that he would do something to cause a revival in his school. And he did. I can't even calculate how many people have told me that they came to Christ because of Sam.

During one long conversation before his death, his girlfriend, Holly, asked Sam how sure he was that he would one day go to heaven.

"I'm one hundred percent sure. How sure are you?"

"I think I'm only eighty percent," she replied.

Sam then shared why he was so sure. One week later, he passed away.

There have been plenty of times I've asked, "Why, Lord? Wasn't there another way Sam could have impacted the kingdom? Why did You take my son when my lifelong goal has always been to serve You in ministry?" I finally realized that I was asking the wrong question. I should have been asking, "Why not?" Many have lost children, siblings, and even their own health and well-being. Who am I to think that it should not happen to me?

I'll never stop missing my child or grieving for the life I once had, but my shoulders have gotten bigger because Jesus helps me carry my cross. My faith has sustained me through periods of intense sadness and depression. Had my roots of faith not been deep, they would have been yanked out.

I cannot pretend to know the mind of God; I can only set my hand in His and trust that my journey will ultimately end in His presence. For that, I am thankful. Without Jesus, I would be lost and bitter.

I miss Sam. I also miss being able to see straight and my ability to get up without pain. I daily surrender these things to God. Regardless of the circumstances surrounding me, I know God loves me and my family. He created us for a future full of hope. Our family will one day be restored just as Sam is completely restored with Jesus right now. I still have challenges, but I'm going to keep working at overcoming them and living this life until it is done. This is my race, and I'm going to run it to the best of my ability.

Kristine's family experienced unexpected blessings after the loss of their son. Many people came to know Jesus and shared their testimonies with others. Despite their devastating loss, this family has a peace that is beyond understanding. They know Sam is safe and happy with the Lord and they will see him again.

True victory isn't waiting for the storm to pass. It's hanging on to God during the storm. He can use every situation to draw us to Himself. While God's healing may not come immediately, or even in this lifetime, it always comes.

7

Your Response Reveals Your Heart

*T*he grocery store is a great place to observe human nature. Not long ago, I was shopping at a supermarket. Having only a few items in my basket, I went to the express lane to check out. A smiling cashier made friendly small talk as she scanned my items. When she couldn't get the scanner to read the barcode on my whole wheat bread, however, she stopped smiling and her face turned red. She spewed uncomplimentary words about another employee, blaming that person for placing the price tag over the barcode.

The way you respond to difficult events provides a snapshot of who you really are. How did you act the last time you experienced a trial? Did you behave in a way that was pleasing to God? Did others see Christ in you? In Matthew 5:14–16, Jesus says, "You are the light of the world. A city set on a hill cannot be hidden. Nor do people light a lamp and put it under a basket, but on a stand, and it gives light to all in the house. In the same way, let your light shine before others, so that they may see your good works and give glory to your Father who is in heaven."

Trials can help us see things about ourselves. They are like spotlights that reveal to us and others where we are spiritually. When I respond to an insult by getting angry, it shows that I have a cer-

71

tain opinion of myself. I expect others to share that opinion, and I am offended when they do not. The way I respond to trials also helps shape my character in the future. Do I choose to slap the person who insulted me? Or do I recognize my anger as a signal that I need to examine myself and learn to love and forgive others as God has forgiven me?

People are like sponges. When sponges get squeezed, what's inside of them comes out. When trials push against us, most of us find that we still have some impurities inside. God's intention is to bring these undesirable qualities into the light so we can see them and apply His transforming power to eliminate them.

Although this process is good for us, it's certainly not pleasant. Nobody likes to experience discomfort. We typically ask God to make things easier by changing our circumstances. When that doesn't happen (or doesn't happen as quickly as we expect), we get frustrated. That doesn't mean God won't change our circumstances eventually, but sometimes He wants our circumstances to change us first.

Are We Changed?

Are you allowing God to use your difficult circumstances to mold you into the person He wants you to be? Paul says, "Do not be conformed to this world, but be transformed by the renewal of your mind, that by testing you may discern what is the will of God, what is good and acceptable and perfect" (Romans 12:2). As Christians, we can choose to respond in godly ways to even the greatest challenges. When we do, the light of Christ shines brightly through us.

Unfortunately, nonbelievers often react to problems better than Christians do. I once witnessed a woman treat a store clerk like a lowly servant. A man standing nearby said, "She must be one of those Christians who go to church every Sunday." I was embarrassed to be counted among "those Christians" that day.

When others cross our paths, we are to be ambassadors for the kingdom of God. God loves the stranger as much as He loves you. He cares for the people at your job, at your church, at your school, and at your home. He has the same compassion for your friends and family members that He has for you.

People need to see God at work in us so they can be influenced by His love. If we don't allow God to shine through us, we could be denying others the opportunity to grow closer to Him.

Through good times and bad, God is with us each step of the way. Isaiah 43:2 says, "When you pass through the waters, I will be with you; and through the rivers, they shall not overwhelm you; when you walk through fire you shall not be burned, and the flame shall not consume you." When we come to grips with the truth that God is in complete control and that He cares about every detail of our lives, we will have a more mature response to our trials.

Jesus is our ultimate example. He was God in the flesh. He could have wielded the power to change His circumstances when things got difficult. Instead, He chose to trust His Father. Even as He pleaded in Gethsemane for the cup of suffering to be taken from Him, Jesus realized the Father's plan was perfect. He knew the cross was the only way to solve the problem of humanity's sin. The Savior's response to suffering was to focus on the Father's will because He trusted that His Father's will was best.

Jesus' prayer in the garden is a poignant example for us. Jesus was honest with the Father about His desire to avoid suffering. Surrender doesn't make you voiceless or passive; it just means that you choose to submit your will to that of the Father. It's what Paul called offering our bodies as living sacrifices (Romans 12:1). As you walk with God in faith, you can continue to grow in your ability to remain steadfast and wait on Him through your trials.

Trust God, Not People

When you trust someone, you feel confident and secure in that relationship. You believe that he or she has the best intentions toward you. When someone you've trusted violates that trust, your ability to trust is broken.

I know of a man who greatly admired his youth director when he was a teen. He wanted to be just like him. As an adult, however, he learned that the youth director was addicted to pornography. Not only did this shred his confidence in the pastor's sterling moral character, but he began to lose trust in the pastor's judgment in other areas as well. Broken trust can be a great reminder that we can't put our trust in people, only in God. The Bible says, "It is better to take refuge in the LORD than to trust in man" (Psalm 118:8).

People will disillusion and disappoint us because all human beings are fallen creatures. Living in a world where trust is so often violated, how can we possibly put our faith in anything wholeheartedly and without fear? Because of what we have experienced, how can we even trust God? The better we know God, the easier it will be for us to respond as Jesus did, with loving trust. Throughout our Christian lives, God will increase our trust in Him. As we keep obeying His Word, His faithfulness will produce good fruit in us.

Learning to Trust Again

I often hear my counseling clients say, "I can't trust God in certain aspects of my life." My response is usually to ask, "Who else in your life have you been unable to trust?" If my client is a woman, I often learn that she had an abusive father or husband. Tragically, that relationship has framed her perspective of God.

We tend to view God through the lens of the experiences we have had with an earthly authority. If we had negative experiences with abusive or negligent earthly leaders, our understanding of God will likely be distorted. That's why trusting God often starts with prayerfully forgiving the offender who first violated our trust or caused us to stop trusting. Once we release that person from the consequences of his or her hurtful actions, we are better able to trust God.

While we may know intellectually that the person in authority is not God, our view of Him and others can still be affected. Until we deal with these negative experiences, we are not free to trust God as we desire. Trust begins with relinquishing control. In general, that is something people don't like to do. In order to trust God, however, you have to let Him take the wheel and let Him drive. You have to release your right to have things your own way. We are called to live like Jesus, entrusting ourselves into the Father's care (1 Peter 2:23). How easy is this for you to do? When times get tough, do you cling more tightly to the steering wheel or do you release control?

You can't expect God to run your life if you're trying to do it yourself. He doesn't share the task. Either He's in charge, or you are. So make the decision to give up the wheel. If your fingers are stuck tight in the driver's position, repent and ask God to move you to the passenger's seat.

Practical Steps to Trusting God

If you have been wounded in the past, you can learn to trust God more. Here are some tips to help pry those fingers loose from the "wheel" and let Jesus take control.

1. Realize that God is not like us.

Hebrews 13:8 says, "Jesus Christ is the same yesterday and today and forever." Unlike people, God has proven Himself completely trustworthy. His actions are based on His love for us, His righteousness, and His full knowledge of the beginning, middle, and end of our trials. Put your trust in who He is and not in how you feel. Emotions can be deceptive. They can draw us away from what is true. If we allow our feelings to control us, we will be focused on our circumstances, not on God.

2. Deny yourself.

In Luke 9:23, Jesus says, "If anyone would come after me, let him deny himself and take up his cross daily and follow me." What does it mean to deny yourself? Start by refusing to give in to those thoughts and urges that are not from God. Resist the inclination to indulge in self-pity or compare yourself to others. Take the focus off yourself and put it on God. Stop dictating to God about when and how to fix your problems, and trust His plan and timing. Are you willing to give up your opinions and desires, trust God's solution and timing, and focus on following Him?

3. Consider your situation from God's perspective.

Our perceptions are shaped by our experiences, our limited knowledge, and the pain we feel. They are molded by our personal desires and ambitions. God, however, sees clearly and completely. Romans 11:33–35 says, "Oh, the depth of the riches and wisdom and knowledge of God! How unsearchable are his judgments and how inscrutable his ways! 'For who has known the mind of the Lord, or who has been his counselor?' 'Or who has given a gift to him that he might be repaid?'"

God is all-knowing and all-powerful. He knows what your future holds. Get into His Word. Find Scriptures that deal with your situation and apply them. Stop asking, "Why me?" and start asking, "What is God trying to teach me?" When we ask the Lord to help us see through His eyes, He can change our perspective. We will trust Him more and begin to better understand His love for us.

4. Be willing to change.

Romans 12:2 says, "Do not be conformed to this world, but be transformed by the renewal of your mind, that by testing you may discern what is the will of God, what is good and acceptable and perfect." By immersing your mind in God's Word and applying its truths, you will be able to discern His will for your life. Even if you need to shift gears and turn around in order to follow God's calling, do it. When you are willing to change directions, you will see God's path open up. Initially, this will probably feel uncomfortable, but if you want to follow God's will, you need to trust Him. You won't be able to do this in your own strength. God gives that strength to you.

5. Ask God for more faith.

Hebrews 11:6 says, "And without faith it is impossible to please him, for whoever would draw near to God must believe that he exists and that he rewards those who seek him." Faith is as vital to your spiritual walk as breathing is to your physical life. However, don't be discouraged if you have limited faith. Jesus said all it takes to move mountains is faith as small as a mustard seed (Matthew 17:20). You can trust God because He loves you, He wants what is best for you, and He is able to meet your needs. God never asks us to do anything by ourselves. When we seek Him, He provides faith, strength, hope, encouragement, and everything else we need.

6. Choose to be thankful rather than complain.

You may not feel like thanking God in the midst of hardship. However, if you choose to thank Him for His faithfulness and provision, you might start seeing His hand in places you didn't before. Psalm 50:23 says, "The one who offers thanksgiving as his sacrifice glorifies me; to one who orders his way rightly I will show the salvation of God!" You will lose hope when you focus on your problems. Instead, concentrate on God's love, His character, and His power, and He will fill you with His strength and make a way for you. Focus on the character and nature of God, and then choose to express your thanks and appreciation to Him, no matter the circumstances. Feelings of gratitude will follow.

Keep Persevering

Even if you apply the ideas listed above, trusting God may not come easily. Over time, as you allow Him to work in you, you will see His faithfulness.

After performing many miracles, from healing the blind and the demon-possessed to bringing people back to life, Jesus told His disciples, "Truly, truly, I say to you, whoever believes in me will also do the works that I do; and greater works than these will he do, because I am going to the Father" (John 14:12). Each problem you face is an opportunity to become more like Jesus. As you begin to see the great things God is doing through you, you will be empowered to do even greater things than Jesus did while on earth.

David's Story

Here's an incredible testimony of a man who chose to let God mold him in the midst of unbelievable tragedy. His story speaks volumes about the power of God to work through even the greatest trials and suffering. It also shows how God can redeem a life—any life—and create beauty from ashes.

I had been up for nearly a week straight doing methamphetamine. I was so sick that I couldn't even stand up. I just lounged in bed using dope. When my wife, Amy, told me she was leaving and taking the kids with her, I snapped. I grabbed my loaded SKS assault rifle, kicked off the safety, and put the weapon under my chin. To Amy's horror, I pulled the trigger.

The bullet shot between my eyes, breaking every bone in my face except for my left eye socket. It blew out nearly all of my teeth, obliterated my nose, and totally disintegrated my mouth. It literally split my face in two. One half was hanging down to my shoulder.

Despite these horrific injuries, I didn't lose consciousness. I remember talking to my mother, who came to our home after a frantic call from the kids. When she screamed out, "Why did you do that?" all I could say was "I'm sorry." I had no idea why I'd shot myself. I had a beautiful wife, six wonderful kids, and a good job, but I was miserable from years of drug addiction.

At Vanderbilt University Medical Center in Nashville, the doctors called me the miracle man. Medical professionals can't explain my recovery. I've had nearly three dozen surgeries. Thirty titanium plates and screws hold my sinuses in and my face together, yet the tests find nothing wrong with my brain. The swelling and trauma it endured should have damaged me beyond repair.

I haven't just been restored to the man I was before I started abusing methamphetamine. I am a new and improved David Parnell. The biggest miracle of all is that I'm clean and sober after twenty-three years of heavy drug use.

At just thirteen, I started using marijuana with my dad to fit in with him and his friends. All of them were drug users. Once I tried methamphetamine, I was hooked, and it was a downward spiral from there. Meth robs people of the ability to love and feel compassion for others. I had no problem hating and wanting to hurt people when I was on it.

Meth robbed me of my health, sent me to prison, and nearly cost me my life. I'm reminded of my bad choices every time I look in the mirror. I could be bitter, but I know God saved me for a reason.

When I woke up in the hospital after my near-death experience, I recommitted my life to Christ. The Lord put it on my heart to share my story with others. I want to do what He asks me to so that I might find favor and never have to go back to that dark place again. Psalm 40:1–3 says, "I waited patiently for the LORD; he inclined to me and heard my cry. He drew me up from the pit of destruction, out of the miry bog, and set my feet upon a rock, making my steps secure. He put a new song in my mouth, a song of praise to our God. Many will see and fear, and put their trust in the LORD."

It's amazing what God has done. He saved me from the horrible pit and put a new song in my mouth. He has blessed me over and over, and I will never stop singing His praises. Much of my story is sad and depressing. My life has had more downs than ups—and many of the downs were self-inflicted. Still, my life story is ultimately one of restoration and recovery.

I have been at death's door numerous times, only to inexplicably survive. I've been involved in several near-fatal car wrecks, been shot at close range, been beaten nearly to death, overdosed more than once, hung myself, and tried to blow off my own head. Many of my friends have lost their lives by things far less extreme.

I know that I'm still here because I have a mission to fulfill. Every morning I wake up with a renewed sense of purpose: to warn others about the dangers of drugs. I am now a full-time motivational speaker. I speak at schools, churches, jails, rehab centers, and community groups about the dangers of methamphetamine and other drugs. My goal is to prevent others from trying methamphetamine and to give hope to those who are already addicted. Ultimately, I want everyone to know how much God loves them.

I've worked hard to break the cycle of addiction and abuse in my own family. My kids have experienced firsthand what drugs and alcohol can do to a person because their dad was a monster.

I used to have a tight circle of druggies, drunks, and violent criminals surrounding me, but now my beautiful family is my gang. My children and my wife are my best friends. We do everything together. Whereas my first home was destructive and dysfunctional, our new home is a sanctuary—a positive, nurturing environment. Our kids are busy with school, sports, and church activities. They don't party like Amy and I did.

The scars on my face are ugly, but they are nothing like the ones I had on the inside. Today, I have hope in my heart. In Luke 7:47, Jesus blessed a sinful woman who had anointed His feet with oil by saying, "Therefore I tell you, her sins, which are many, are forgiven—for she loved much." Likewise, my many sins have been forgiven. For the first time I have a future full of promise. No matter what tomorrow brings, I know God loves me. It was brutal hand-to-hand combat, but good finally triumphed over evil and slew the dragon.

If you would like to know more about David's story, you may visit his website at www.FacingTheDragon.org.

Trials can come from our own errors and those of others. David didn't choose to have a father who used drugs, but he chose to use them himself as a teen and an adult. Yet no trial is too large for God to bring restoration.

We can be certain that David's childhood left him with scars. It left an impact on his wife and family too, even though that impact is not detailed in this account. Too often, stories like this are oversimplified. It would be naïve to think his children don't have scars too. The point is to understand there is light at the end of the tunnel, no matter what darkness you face. If David and his family can experience restoration, so can you.

Romans 8:18 says, "For I consider that the sufferings of this present time are not worth comparing with the glory that is to be revealed to us." While this verse speaks of the glory on the other side of this life—in heaven—it can be applied to life on the other side of a difficult trial as well. The scars and some of the pain may persist, but there is joy in seeing that God understands and knowing He is with us.

In the end, our souls, and our love for God and others, will be the only parts of us that remain. Focus on what truly matters. Ask God to use every situation in your life—past, present, and future—for His glory.

When We Don't Understand

O ne beautiful spring, I hiked a 14,000-foot mountain in Colorado. After hours of steep climbing, I sat at the top and relaxed as the light gray clouds provided a cool mist. I closed my eyes for a while. When I opened them, the clouds had begun to clear, and a double rainbow filled the sky with vibrancy. The colors were so rich that I desperately wanted to reach out and touch them across the top of the mountain. I could scarcely believe that such a beautiful thing was not an illusion. It was amazing, and not once did I question, "Why? Why did God put this double rainbow in my life?" I didn't feel the need to analyze the beautiful sight nor try to move or change it.

When times are good and life is lovely, we rarely question God or fight against our circumstances. When we encounter suffering, though, the first question that enters our mind is, "Why? Why me? Why now?" We are overcome by the need to know why God would allow such pain. The truth is, God doesn't give us explanations for everything that happens, but He does give us important truths in His Word. He asks that we have faith in Him. Whether our hearts are filled with wonder or sorrow, He tells us that we can trust in His love for us. To give us confidence in Him, God provides us with the testimonies of faithful people who have gone before us—people who have also endured pain and have received no explanation for their suffering yet have remained in the center of God's will.

In fifty-two chapters, the book of Jeremiah tells about God's heart toward His people. The prophet Jeremiah was appointed by God as His spokesperson (Jeremiah 1:4–5) and spent decades giving God's messages to people who would not change (Jeremiah 25:3). Being a chosen servant of God was the greatest honor Jeremiah could have received, yet he suffered trials even in the midst of God's blessing. Jeremiah carried God's wrenching messages to his people, saw the messages have no effect, and then received scorn and hatred from those he was trying to help. He told God, "I have become a laughingstock all the day; everyone mocks me . . . For I hear many whispering. Terror is on every side! 'Denounce him! Let us denounce him!' say all my close friends, watching for my fall. 'Perhaps he will be deceived; then we can overcome him and take our revenge on him'" (Jeremiah 20:7, 10). Can you hear the anguish in Jeremiah's voice?

God does not change Jeremiah's situation or give him a more positive message. Nor do the people begin loving Jeremiah. Yet the prophet's hope and peace remain in God rather than in his circumstances or in others' attitudes. Jeremiah testifies, "But the LORD is with me as a dread warrior . . . Sing to the LORD; praise the LORD!" (Jeremiah 20:11, 13). Jeremiah's life is a beautiful example of trusting in, acknowledging, and obeying God through difficulties. If we understood God's reasons for every trial we faced, we wouldn't need faith. Yet we know that He is with us and for us, and that if we trust in Jesus as Savior, our eternal destinies are secure.

Proverbs 3:5–6 says, "Trust in the LORD with all your heart, and do not lean on your own understanding. In all your ways acknowledge him, and he will make straight your paths." This passage says that we are to trust in the Lord with *all* our hearts, not just parts of them. By drawing a contrast, it tells us that understanding is different from trust. The end of verse six promises that God will make straight our paths. God never promised us an easy path, but He promises a straight one if we acknowledge Him in all our ways, even through the trials we don't understand.

Looking for Reasons

I was born with epilepsy. From my earliest recollection, I had a seizure at least once a week. Other kids didn't understand what was happening and made fun of me. I tried numerous medications over the years, but none really worked. To make matters worse, the medication caused intense depression and anger, which often caused me to contemplate suicide. These emotional side effects were almost worse than the seizures. Even today, I need medication. This medication controls the seizures, but I still sometimes experience depression and drowsiness.

I don't understand why God created me this way. If I am honest, I would say I wish I never had to deal with health problems. However, the Bible says that I am "fearfully and wonderfully made" (Psalm 139:14). God uses my health to draw me closer to Him. Because of my challenges, I pray often, asking God for strength, wisdom, and help rather than following my temptation to live independently of Him.

Perhaps your struggle isn't physical. Maybe it's emotional, relational, or spiritual. We all experience pain and the discomforts of living in a fallen world. As we do, God asks us to trade short-term suffering for long-term gain. It's a bit like getting a flu shot. We accept a needle prick now to avoid fever, dizziness, and chills later. In much the same way, God allows us to experience seasons of trial in order to gain long-term benefit. Godly character lasts forever, and molding this character matters much more to God than our fleeting earthly comfort. Our suffering may feel like it lasts forever, but in comparison to true eternity, it is only the blink of an eye.

Someday Satan will be vanquished, and there will be no more death, mourning, crying, or pain (Revelation 21:4).

Sometimes God allows us to suffer short-term pain not for our own benefit, but for someone else's. For example, if you donate a kidney, you experience temporary pain and inconvenience for the long-term health of another. Similarly, God might allow you to go through a trial to prepare you to meet the needs of someone you may not even know yet. When Jesus died on the cross for our sins, He suffered staggering short-term pain for our long-term gain of eternal life.

God allows us to experience affliction, but He never abandons us to endure suffering alone. He provides us with solace and comfort through it all. Psalm 46:10 offers great wisdom for the times we undergo hardship we cannot comprehend. It says, "Be still, and know that I am God." Being still doesn't imply that we stop our lives to pray around the clock. It means that we stop striving to reach our own objectives and are willing for God to accomplish what He wants to do. Ultimately, stillness is being open to hearing God speak to us.

When we allow our souls to be still, we will be able to hear the Spirit of God reminding us how well He knows us and how much He loves us. In John 14:27, Jesus says, "Peace I leave with you; my peace I give to you. Not as the world gives do I give to you. Let not your hearts be troubled, neither let them be afraid." This kind of peace can only come from God.

Jesus offers us peace because He knows how desperately we need it. We might think for a time that our most urgent need is for our situations to change or for our hurt to subside. However, God's peace helps us to have the right perspective and enables us to act according to His will. The soft, quiet voice of the Holy Spirit gives us comfort. Listening with a still mind and a ready heart brings peace in the midst of pain.

I Can't Complain

When suffering occurs, our initial reaction is to complain. We aren't alone. People have been complaining for thousands of years. The Israelites were no strangers to complaining either.

The Israelites wandered in the desert for forty years. Whenever they found themselves in uncomfortable situations, they whined to their leader, Moses. They wanted water, so God gave them water. Then they wanted food, so God sent manna. They wanted meat, so God gave them quail. They soon grew tired of that too. They were never satisfied. The Israelites were also fearful, causing them to sin against God by not trusting Him. They feared the wrath of the Egyptians. They feared the unknowns of their new freedom. They feared what was ahead and started missing what they'd left behind. They accused God of bringing them out to the desert to die. They worried about starving to death. They dreaded entering the Promised Land because they feared the inhabitants, whom they had heard were like giants. They never fully relied upon God's power and protection. As a result, the Israelites rejected God's gifts of provision and a new homeland.

Although it is easy to condemn the Israelites for their lack of faith, we do the same thing. When we cannot see behind God's curtain, we tend to embrace discontentment, disbelief, or fear. The temptation is to complain, but this serves no productive or godly purpose. Ultimately, complaining is a form of rebellion. It limits God's power because in our mutiny against God's ways, we block out the one perfect source of help—God Himself. Perhaps this is why, in his letter to the Philippians, Paul wrote, "Do all things without grumbling or disputing, that you may be blameless and innocent, children of God without blemish in the midst of a crooked and twisted generation, among whom you shine as lights in the world" (Philippians 2:14–15).

I know a woman named Helen who went through a trial that lasted more than a decade. She prayed repeatedly for God to bring healing to her situation, but the trial lasted so long that her prayers felt stale, insincere, and hollow. She would lie in bed at night, wanting to pray—knowing she needed to pray—but she couldn't make herself ask God to change her circumstances one more time. Rather than continue to pray without sincerity, she stopped praying altogether.

After about six months of wallowing in self-pity, God opened her spiritual eyes to see that prayer isn't always about asking for things; it's also thanking God for things. Realizing that prayer was the only hope she had, Helen began to thank God for all the blessings in her life. After several days of praying nothing but prayers of gratitude, Helen began to recognize God's presence in her situation in a way she hadn't before. Instead of perceiving God as having abandoned her, she saw Him as an ever-present help. She started to comprehend how He had blessed her, provided for her, and comforted her even in the midst of her painful circumstances. Shifting to prayers of gratitude helped Helen refocus on God's character. She learned that she didn't always need to understand God's reasons or purposes in order to trust Him.

The Israelites would have done well to learn this lesson. Fundamentally, their constant complaining was a reflection of ungratefulness. They even complained about the manna, saying that they hated eating it. This is incredible when one considers the Bible says manna was angels' food. Instead of treasuring this precious gift, they complained that they wanted meat instead. They did not recognize the beauty of God's miraculous supply.

Can you relate to the Israelites? I can. We may not have wandered in a physical desert for forty years, but most likely, we have been lost in a spiritual desert at one time or another. Sometimes we get lost for years, if not decades. We are tired and weary. Our spiritual life seems stale and dry. When this happens, it is easy to slip into an attitude of ingratitude. We experience a lack of gratitude when we assume that the Provider does not have our best interests at heart and owes us something better. The ungrateful person's reasoning goes like this: "If God truly cared about me, He would give me what I want." The reality is, if God gave us what we preferred rather than what is best for us, we would miss out on the greater blessings He desires to bring about through the circumstances He has allowed.

God never fails to answer His people when they humble their hearts and call out to Him for help. As we grow in spiritual maturity, we come to understand that His help doesn't always come in the form we expect. We must be willing to serve God even when our circumstances are not what we would choose. The ultimate goal of our lives is not self-satisfaction but worshipping God and being conformed to His image.

Suffering for Service

When trials overwhelm us and we cannot make sense of what is happening, how can we reframe our thinking in a more productive way? We can start by remembering that trials shape our character. Paul told the Christian church in Rome, "Not only that, but we rejoice in our sufferings, knowing that suffering produces endurance, and endurance produces character, and character produces hope" (Romans 5:3–4).

Trials also prepare us for service to others. We are better able to minister to those around us if we have gone through similar situations. If we don't harden our hearts and become bitter, our experiences give us empathy, compassion, and a perspective we might not otherwise have had. How many times have you been able to encourage someone with a story of how you lived through a challenge? How many times have you retold an instance in which

God saved you or came through for you? That can be extremely meaningful to someone who's on a similar path to your own.

Sally was shocked when her husband left her for a young beauty. Although Sally knew the Lord and walked closely with Him, she was shattered. She struggled to raise their two young children alone, especially after she lost her job and her finances crumbled. Then her health deteriorated. Sally prayed every day that God would change her husband's heart and repair the damage that had been done to her family. One day, before her prayers were realized, Sally's car was hit by a semi-truck. She was killed instantly. Faced with single fatherhood, her husband ended his adulterous relationship and moved back home to take care of his grieving children. He even started taking them to church.

God did not cause Sally's fatal accident. However, He used this tragedy to bring her husband to his senses. Sally's suffering is over, and she is now basking in the endless joy of her King. Her husband has turned away from his path of destruction, and her children now have a legacy of two believing parents.

Humanly speaking, this story is not just. Why should a faithful woman have to die? Why should the children lose their mother? From an earthly perspective, these questions have no satisfying answers. Sometimes we come to understand our pain in retrospect. Other times we can see some reasons, but these reasons feel inadequate for the degree of suffering involved. In these instances, all we can do is trust that our loving Heavenly Father is accomplishing things that we cannot see.

Whenever we observe or experience what we believe is undeserved suffering and think, *Why?*, we should look to the cross, where the greatest suffering of all time occurred. Our innocent Savior became sin on our behalf. He suffered and died in our place. In the midst of His unfathomable agony, Jesus cried out, "My God, my God, why have you forsaken me?" (Mark 15:34). Yet through this most undeserved and intense of all torture, God brought about the greatest good—the free gift of eternal life. Because of Jesus' affliction, we can have hope. We can have hope, not only in eternal life, but in knowing that we have a God who identifies with our pain. Moreover, we can know that if God brought about the greatest good from the greatest evil, He will bring about goodness from our anguish that is beyond what we can imagine. We can trust Him that the greater the trial we are experiencing now, the greater the good He will bring about later.

Whether trials come as the result of our own sin, someone else's sin, or simply from living in a fallen world, God can and will use them for our good and His glory.

Be Prepared

If we want to stand strong in adversity tomorrow, we need to start laying the foundation today. We can prepare ourselves for times of suffering by developing a capacity to face trouble with courage and handle disappointment with hope. If you have trouble doing this, here are a few ideas to get you started.

1. Learn from the examples of others.

First and foremost, we can learn about God's love and sovereignty through studying the Scriptures. James 5:10–11 says, "As an example of suffering and patience, brothers, take the prophets who spoke in the name of the Lord. Behold, we consider those blessed who remained steadfast. You have heard of the steadfastness of Job, and you have seen the purpose of the Lord, how the Lord is compassionate and merciful." We can find encouragement by reading about godly men and women in the Bible as well as those in historical and modern times. God has given us excellent role models of faith.

2. Get to know God's character.

Really getting to know God doesn't happen overnight. It occurs gradually as we read God's Word, communicate with Him in prayer, and walk with Him daily.

God wants us to know Him intimately. In Jeremiah 9:23–24, we read, "Thus says the LORD: 'Let not the wise man boast in his wisdom, let not the mighty man boast in his might, let not the rich man boast in his riches, but let him who boasts boast in this, that he understands and knows me, that I am the LORD who practices steadfast love, justice, and righteousness in the earth. For in these things I delight, declares the LORD.'" A close relationship with God is worth far more than riches, success, or happy circumstances.

We can get to know God through studying His Word, praying, obeying His commands, and fellowshipping with others. We also get to know Him by intentionally listening for Him to speak to our hearts. As we put aside the clamor in our minds, we can open ourselves to commune with God.

As with any relationship, spending time with God will grow our love and commitment to Him.

3. Refuse to complain.

Whenever you are tempted to complain, replace grumbling with praise. Praise God for His goodness and mercy, which never changes, no matter what happens in or around us (Hebrews 13:8). We can still be honest with God and pour out our hearts to Him, but if we put all of our concerns to rest at God's feet, we will find peace.

Paul told the Philippians, "Finally, my brothers, rejoice in the Lord" (Philippians 3:1). God wants us to praise Him in every circumstance, not just when things are going well. Since our natural inclination is to focus on the negative, we must sometimes be reminded to rejoice (Philippians 4:4).

When we complain about our circumstances, we tend to become so overwhelmed that we are blind to the positive things in our lives.

On the other hand, if we make a determined effort to replace our complaints with praise for our many blessings, we will be able to rejoice in God's constant love, mercy, and faithfulness no matter the situation.

4. Change your requests.

Instead of begging God to remove your trial, ask what He wants you to learn through it. What might God be doing in you and through you? Difficulties tend to reveal our unpleasant qualities. Perhaps there is something in your character, behavior, or thought patterns that God wants to change. Times of suffering have the potential to be our greatest seasons of growth if we repent of any exposed sin and ask God to renew our minds.

The Israelites endured many trials and challenges during their forty years of wandering in the wilderness. We can learn a valuable lesson from their mistakes. Scripture says, "And you shall remember the whole way that the LORD your God has led you these forty years in the wilderness, that he might humble you, testing you to know what was in your heart, whether you would keep his commandments or not. And he humbled you and let you hunger and fed you with manna, which you did not know, nor did your fathers know, that he might make you know that man does not live by bread alone, but man lives by every word that comes from the mouth of the LORD" (Deuteronomy 8:2–3).

The Israelites' temporary trials offered opportunities for eternal lessons and for changes in their hearts. They learned that their only hope was in dependence on God. It's important for us to learn that as well.

5. Live out whatever God shows you.

Put the lessons you are learning into practice. God will honor your choice to walk in faith. James 1:22–25 says, "But be doers of the word, and not hearers only, deceiving yourselves. For if anyone is a hearer of the word and not a doer, he is like a man who looks intently at his natural face in a mirror. For he looks at himself and goes away and at once forgets what he was like. But the one who looks into the perfect law, the law of liberty, and perseveres, being no hearer who forgets but a doer who acts, he will be blessed in his doing." Learning important truths won't help us if we don't apply them to our lives. When you hear God's correction, be sure to respond to it.

Ask God to make you aware of His Holy Spirit speaking to you through Bible study, prayer, godly counsel, and the promptings of your conscience. Be prepared to change your course of action based on His directives.

Every trial we experience can be viewed as an opportunity for spiritual growth. When we take the focus off ourselves and place it on our Father, we begin to see things from His point of view. We begin to take an eternal perspective rather than an earthly one. Going through difficult experiences enables us to remove our spiritual training wheels so we can mature and grow in the likeness of Christ.

Kirk's Story

Sometimes we neglect to look at the long-term consequences of our actions and behavior. Kirk suffered from brokenness that stemmed from losing a child. This is the story of a man who, even though he didn't understand his situation, decided to trust in the One who did. Look for the treasure of his growing trust as you read his testimony.

The latter part of my senior year of high school, something unexpected happened—I got my girlfriend pregnant. There were things I wanted to do right after high school, and being a father was not one of them. How was I going to support a family? I had really messed up.

After graduation, we got married, and I moved in with my in-laws. I made just over minimum wage working for a pharmacy delivering medications to nursing homes around the state. Before long, I went to work in the production department of the manufacturing company where my dad worked. I worked twelve-hour night shifts on the production floor, making $9.00 to $11.00 an hour plus insurance, while my wife worked at McDonald's as a lead, making around $6.00 an hour.

I will never forget the morning of February 13, 1997. I was at work when I got a phone call from my wife. She said her parents were rushing her to Freeway Medical because of problems with the baby. When my parents and I got to the clinic, we got the news—our baby had died! I broke down in a way I never had before. How and why could such a thing have happened? Why did God allow it?

That day was the longest of my life. As if such news weren't horrible enough, we now had to go through induction and delivery of our lifeless child. I paced anxiously in the waiting room while my wife labored for hours before she finally gave birth. I remember being in the room when they told her to push one last time. Instead of the usual cries of a newborn baby, the room was deafeningly silent. Kaitlyn Ashley was beautiful and near term at eight and a half months. I held her for some time, just looking at her through tear-filled eyes. When they came to take her away for an autopsy, the pain I felt nearly crushed me.

The funeral was held a few days after her birth, and the burial was the hardest thing I had ever had to deal with. When I saw Kaitlyn in that tiny coffin being lowered into the ground, I wished I could die too. I was full of anger, bitterness, and confusion, with no idea how I would make it through. I was convinced it was all because we had sexual relations outside of marriage. I blamed myself and my wife for the loss of our baby.

Depression quickly set in and the pain remained with me for years. Believing God was responsible for our pain, I rebelled against Him and wondered if our marriage would last. Fortunately, my wife is very forgiving, and after a time, I finally came back to God in repentance. That is just one of the awesome things about God. He's all about second chances, third chances, and more because He loves us so much.

In time my wife got pregnant again, but had a miscarriage. She was classified as prone to high-risk pregnancy, but God did something miraculous. On August 25, 1998, we brought home a little girl named Kayla Lynn. We considered her our miracle child. On March 18, 2003, we had another little girl named Katherine Nicole, and then on September 16, 2008, we brought home one more, Kassidy Renee. I never anticipated having three such beautiful little girls. God truly blessed me!

As I look back, it's clear that God carried me through Kaitlyn's death, the single most trying circumstance of my life. There was no way I could have gone through it without Him. He has seen me through other losses since then. Will I see Kaitlyn again? You bet I will!

> Even though I sinned against God, He forgave me and still loves me with an everlasting love. To this day, He pours out undeserved blessings on me and my family. I know that as long as I'm alive, I will face struggles and heartaches, but God will be there for me, strengthening me and making me into the person He destined me to be as I stand in faith and put my trust in Him.

It's difficult to imagine the pain Kirk and his wife went through in losing their first two children. This story of beauty from ashes is made even more poignant because of the great strengthening of their faith. God showed them His love over and over again in the birth of three beautiful daughters. The happy ending is not only the growth of Kirk's family, but also the restoration of his heart to the Lord. When he returned to God, his relationship with his Heavenly Father was restored. Then no matter what God allowed into his life, he was in a place of trust and peace.

When Peter saw Jesus walking on the water in the midst of a storm, he exercised tremendous faith as he stepped out of that boat (Matthew 14:28–31). Perhaps we only discover what real faith is when we decide to step out of our vessel of fleshly reason and walk above the wind and waves of our circumstances. We can rise higher than our trials when we place our trust wholly in Jesus.

No matter what circumstances life brings, we can keep walking toward Jesus, maintaining full confidence in God.

Forks in the Road

esus invested three years in Judas Iscariot just as He did the other eleven disciples, yet Judas chose to betray Him. Despite all the miracles Judas witnessed, it appears that he never believed Jesus was the Messiah. Perhaps Judas didn't accept Jesus for who He was because like many Jews at the time, he was looking for a political Messiah. As prophesied, Jesus was "the stone that the builders [the leaders of that day] rejected" (Psalm 118:22; Matthew 21:42).

We don't know why Judas betrayed Jesus; however, we do know that Satan entered Judas and influenced him (Luke 22:3). We also know that, as the money keeper for the disciples, Judas kept some of the funds for himself (John 12:6). When he was betraying Jesus, he bargained with the chief priests for a bounty (Matthew 26:14–15). After Judas handed Jesus over to be crucified, however, the thirty pieces of silver for which he had negotiated meant nothing to him. He was so full of remorse that he returned the money (Matthew 27:3). In the end, Judas was unable to live with his choices and committed suicide.

We, too, can fall into deep pits if we chase things we selfishly desire instead of walking toward God with a loving and repentant heart. We suffer consequences for not following the Lord. But if we have a change of heart and walk away from those bad decisions, God will use our new choices for good, even though some of the consequences may remain.

Without godly wisdom, our best efforts can lead us astray. James writes, "If any of you lacks wisdom, let him ask God, who gives generously to all without reproach, and it will be given him. But let him ask in faith, with no doubting, for the one who doubts is like a wave of the sea that is driven and tossed by the wind" (James 1:5–6). Believing God doesn't just mean intellectual knowledge, but acting on what we know in obedience. Not believing leads to aimless wandering. One day we may think we should choose one way, then the next day we think we should go another. Once we have received wisdom from God on a situation, we are responsible for putting it into practice. God desires that we seek His will, then follow through with obeying it.

Paul issued a warning and promise about godly versus ungodly choices in his letter to the churches in southern Galatia: "Do not be deceived: God is not mocked, for whatever one sows, that will he also reap. For the one who sows to his own flesh will from the flesh reap corruption, but the one who sows to the Spirit will from the Spirit reap eternal life" (Galatians 6:7–8). I believe God would have forgiven Judas Iscariot if he had repented and sought forgiveness, but he still may have had to experience the consequences of his choice.

Even if consequences are not immediately apparent, we will eventually come to regret our foolish decisions.

If It's Dumb, Why Do We Do It?

If we understand that we reap what we sow, why do we continue to make decisions that don't line up with God's Word or plan for us? Perhaps we think our choices will make us happy, and they might for a while. Or we may want to impress others, look good, or appear important. However, God's ways are ultimately best for us. His ways lead to good, and our ways lead to destruction.

Sometimes we know we shouldn't do something, but we move forward anyway. Maybe we think we can get away with it. Perhaps we are carried away by impatience or lust. Or maybe our consciences have become seared, and we no longer feel the weight of our actions. Regardless, such choices suggest that we are either more interested in worldly pursuits than spiritual ones or that we choose to do what is easier rather than what is right.

I have counseled several couples who divorced because it seemed like the easy way out at the time, but later they were filled with deep regret. Michelle, for example, was proud to be a pastor's wife early in her marriage. As the years went by, however, she became increasingly upset that her husband spent so much time at church events rather than with her and their three teenage children. At one point, she developed hives and had difficulty breathing. When she consulted her physician, he could find no physical cause for her symptoms and said they must be stress-related. This diagnosis increased Michelle's annoyance with her husband. Blaming him for her ill health, she divorced him. She married and divorced two more times. Finally, at age seventy, she wished she had stuck it out with her first husband. Because of her shortsighted decision, Michelle never got to see what God could have done in her marriage had she chosen to trust and follow Him.

In the midst of trials, we can make unwise decisions that make our problems worse. Proverbs 14:12 and 16:25 state, "There is a way that seems right to a man, but its end is the way to death." Perhaps you have made a choice that seemed right at the time but in the end was wrong. Don't give up hope! No matter what you've done or how terrible things seem, God can use every bad decision for your good and His glory. Surrendering to Him now may not remove the consequences you're experiencing, but your future will be brighter than it would have been otherwise. Each choice you make is an opportunity to show either what God has already taught you or what you have yet to learn.

We often make wiser decisions when we give situations time to develop instead of acting too quickly. Don't be in a hurry to make big choices that have far-reaching consequences. One of my clients, Shelly, thought she needed to have a perfect house so guests would love to come and visit. She bought a big, new home and filled it with expensive furniture. At first the payments were manageable, but then her hours at work were drastically cut. She no longer had enough money to pay the bills, including the mortgage, and foreclosure seemed like the only option. While she had no control over her hours at work, she could have avoided her financial struggles by being wiser with her purchases. Rather than purchasing a large house and fancy furniture to impress friends and neighbors, she would have been better off buying a house that fit her needs rather than her wants. Oftentimes our desire for the latest and best gadgets causes us to take on needless debt. The Bible says, "The rich rules over the poor, and the borrower is the slave of the lender" (Proverbs 22:7). That is what happened in Shelly's case.

Before you make an important decision, especially in the midst of a trial, ask yourself these questions:

- Is this decision for my benefit or for the glory of God? (1 Corinthians 10:31)
- Does it line up with Scripture? (Psalm 119:11)
- Have I sought wise counsel? (Proverbs 15:22)
- Have I prayed about it? (Proverbs 2:3–5)
- What are my motives? (James 4:3)
- What long-term consequences could I reap? (Proverbs 21:5)
- Will it strengthen or hinder my relationship with Christ? (Ephesians 1:17)

Taking this short inventory can help you avoid heartache.

When you pray about your decisions, take the time to listen to what God is saying in response. Be ready to accept His answer, even if it's not the one you want. Trust God's leadership and be willing to step outside your comfort zone to enable Him to work.

Timing Is Everything

While it's often important to wait before making a decision, there is also a time to act. Ecclesiastes 3:1 says, "For everything there is a season, and a time for every matter under heaven." Take the example of Stan and Lisa. They dated for a long time, loved one another, and agreed on many vital things about life. Yet something held Stan back from asking Lisa to marry him. Eventually he realized it was a fear of commitment. After they'd dated for several years, Lisa wanted to know if the relationship was going somewhere. Despite the length of their relationship, Stan said he still wasn't ready for marriage and needed more time. When another year passed without a proposal, Lisa left him. By refusing to make a decision, Stan had lost the love of his life.

Sometimes, as in Stan and Lisa's example, we don't make a decision because we think not acting is safer. However, not making a decision *is* making a decision—and that decision is usually driven by fear. If the Bible, godly counsel, and prayer are leading you in a particular direction, don't be afraid to move. When God tells us to be still, He wants our hearts and minds to be in a place of quietness and surrender so we can hear Him. But when He leads us to act, we need to act. Continuing to wait reveals a lack of faith and can reap consequences of its own.

God's resolutions to our problems don't always come right away. We may have to wait days, months, or even years. When this happens, it's important to remember that the timing is as much a part of His plan as the answer.

Will You Go Your Own Way?

God's answer may also involve more people than just you. Although you might be ready for Him to move, God may be using your situation in someone else's life in a way that you cannot see. That's why we need the wisdom only He can give.

Many people have jobs that involve dealing with difficult people, and going to work is a challenge. When a boss is demanding or a customer or client is unkind, it's easy to rationalize being rude in return or avoiding the person who is a source of discomfort. It might even be easier to quit the job. However, people are watching the way we respond to challenges. Instead of seeking retaliation for wrongs committed against us or trying to remove ourselves from difficult situations, we must commit to loving and praying for those with whom we work.

I know a woman who chose to pray for the unkind people in her office and reach out to them with love and kindness. Eventually they noticed something different about her and were drawn to the light of Jesus they saw in her. In time, her boss became less demanding and her coworkers became friendlier. Of course, we shouldn't be kind to others just to get what we want, but out of obedience to God. This will strengthen us in our walk with Him.

Exhibiting patience during life's trials isn't easy, especially when everything inside us screams for a situation to be resolved as soon as possible. But even in the most challenging circumstances, God can help us love those who have hurt us. In the midst of mistreatment, we can demonstrate His amazing love by returning kindness for persecution. When we offer grace to those who least deserve it, people see Christ in us. We may even find an opportunity to share the gospel with the perpetrator.

Paul wrote, "Be kind to one another, tenderhearted, forgiving one another, as God in Christ forgave you" (Ephesians 4:32). That kind of attitude is only possible when we give up bitterness and let God soften our wounded hearts.

A single mother named Leslie struggled to make ends meet and had to work two jobs to provide for her children. When her brother offered to care for her girls at no charge, she felt he was a godsend. She was grateful they would be with family. As the years went by, however, her daughters became increasingly angry and silent toward their mother. Although Leslie didn't know it at the time, her brother was molesting them. One daughter sought the guidance of a Christian counselor and began to heal from the wounds caused by her uncle's abuse. In the process, she forgave her uncle. She also forgave her mother for leaving her and her sister with him. When Leslie's daughter was able to tell her what happened, their relationship began to blossom. Sadly, the other daughter held on to bitterness. Because she has refused to forgive, she hasn't been free to grow. This has caused problems in all of her relationships.

Bitterness is a powerful, destructive emotion. But we can return to a place of peace through forgiveness and repentance. We must let God give us the grace to forgive those who have hurt us. The Bible says, "See to it that no one fails to obtain the grace of God; that no 'root of bitterness' springs up and causes trouble, and by it many become defiled" (Hebrews 12:15). Bitterness doesn't only affect us. It affects all of our relationships and the people we come in contact with. If you have chosen bitterness, confess your bad choices and negative attitudes and ask God to forgive you through the blood of Jesus Christ. If you have offended or hurt others because of your anger or decisions, seek their forgiveness. Grace, strength, comfort, and provision await those who walk after the Spirit of God, even when forgiveness doesn't come naturally.

Aleta's Story

The following testimony shows how limited our human understanding can be. God knows the end from the beginning, but we often cannot comprehend how He can make something beautiful from tragedy because we haven't yet seen the end of our stories. Aleta made poor choices. She succumbed to substance abuse and battled an eating disorder, both consequences of living in a fallen world. Yet when she gave her life to Christ, she was restored and given a new purpose: to point others dealing with addiction to the Great Healer.

⁓

I was born and raised in Pennsylvania, the youngest of three children, including two older brothers. I am the family's only adopted child. I grew up in a small community and was always considered an outsider. Because my parents tried to help smooth the way for me, they were very lenient. I was a very strong-willed child, and at the age of fourteen, I rebelled against my parents' authority.

From an early age, I learned how to get my own way. I became adept at manipulating my parents and situations to my benefit. In my early teens, I became very secretive and began to experiment with alcohol. By the time I was sixteen, I was drinking and partying on a regular basis.

In college I became obsessed with my appearance and what others thought of me. This resulted in my first encounter with bulimia. Two months into my freshman year, I met a guy named Jerry in a bar. We became regulars of the bar scene.

A few months later, my parents flew to California on vacation and were killed in a plane crash. As an immature eighteen-year-old, I found it extremely difficult to deal with their deaths. It took a week for my parents' bodies to be returned for burial, and I had no one to talk to during that time. The rest of my family had turned their backs on me. Having lost the only two people whom I felt really loved me, I was in shock. I felt abandoned and alone. I had nightmares and wanted nothing more than to escape my pain.

Jerry was the only person who cared enough to help me. He proposed to me three months after my parents died. Even though he had been wonderful to me, I thought he just felt sorry for me. I had nowhere else to go, so I married him. I was sure that if I started a whole new life, I would be fine.

Not long after we were married, an old schoolmate introduced me to marijuana. I introduced marijuana to Jerry, and we became regular users.

Six months later, Jerry was in a serious auto accident on his way home from a bar. I was in the car behind him and was the first one to the scene. He was in critical condition for three weeks. Once more I was traumatized, so I reverted back to my old eating disorder. I was terrified that I was going to lose Jerry and that he would leave me all alone.

After almost a year of plastic surgeries, Jerry and I returned to partying. We became involved with heavy drugs and had so many parties that the local police knew our address by heart. About that time, I became pregnant with our first child. We were so paranoid about getting caught with drugs that we decided to relocate just to get away from the authorities. We loaded up our belongings and moved to Fort Lauderdale, Florida.

It was then that I was introduced to cocaine. It seemed to take away all the pain of the past, so it became my drug of choice. Cocaine became a daily preoccupation, more than I can even describe. Two-and-a-half years later, I became pregnant with our second child, a son who was born addicted to cocaine.

Jerry's parents had moved from Pennsylvania to Arizona and encouraged us to move there as well. When the children were eighteen months and four years old, we left Florida and moved out West to be near his family.

Jerry went into business with his family and was gone many long hours, leaving me alone with the two children. I became depressed and comforted myself with drugs.

A neighbor befriended me, and she told me that God really did exist and that He loved me. I couldn't believe that a God who loved me would take away those whom I loved. She challenged me to believe, and she invited me to a conference in Texas. While I was there, we attended a church where I cried out to God to reveal Himself to me. I was born again that night, and it was a radical turning point in my life. From that moment on, I never touched cocaine again.

When we returned home, my neighbor gave me a Bible and told me to read everything written in red. She said those were the words of Jesus. In six months, I fell deeply in love with Jesus and was convinced that He had forgiven all my sins, both past and present. I realized that I was chosen by God, and because Jesus loved me, He would never abandon me.

It took three years before I finally started going to church. One Sunday, Jerry went with me. He went forward and received Jesus. He let go of alcohol and drugs, and immediately began to clean up his life.

Shortly after, we became involved in the church and found wonderful friends who mentored us. In 1985, we moved to

Missouri, where we bought a business and helped a small church get started.

Jerry and I had a desire to help others in the drug culture from which God had freed us. We volunteered with a ministry at our church called Addiction Recovery. Eventually, we became the directors. A few years later, we changed the name of the ministry to Living Free and began using materials from the Turning Point/Living Free Ministry in Chattanooga, Tennessee.

Since that time, we have seen many people set free from various life-controlling issues through the power of Jesus Christ. God has opened the door for us to minister in two correctional centers. For several years, I also spoke at Ruth Graham & Friends conferences, helping others who struggle with drug and alcohol addictions.

It has truly been a miracle to be a part of what God can do in and through one broken life.

God worked through Aleta's circumstances and ultimately used them for His glory. Her story demonstrates that God is indeed a loving and forgiving God who is slow to anger and abounding in steadfast love (Psalm 103:8). He wants to not only be Lord of our lives, but also use our lives to minister to others and help bring them to salvation and repentance.

Each of us has a divinely appointed purpose on earth. Are you willing to turn your life and decisions over to God? If so, you can choose to follow the direction He has laid out for you rather than going your own way. You can live a godly life according to His guidelines instead of conforming to the world. You can either wait or act in obedience according to His direction. Your choices can have far-reaching consequences for good or evil. Choose to trust Him.

1.0

Muscle-Building Adversity

*E*xercising is not my favorite activity. Fitness enthusiasts often express how they like working out, but as far as I am concerned, there is nothing fun about it. I once purchased a power walking DVD. The label assured me that I would become trim and healthy if I just followed the program. That sounded simple enough. I popped in the DVD, which began with easy walking steps. I compliantly pointed my toes and moved my arms to the music. Then the steps got more complicated, and I started to get warm. Halfway through the disc, I was breathing heavily and my makeup sweated off. I opened the back door to get some relief, not caring that it was windy and 40 degrees outside. I wasn't sure I would make it to the end, but somehow I finished the whole workout.

After doing the routine several more times in the days that followed, it got easier. As a result of suffering through the exercises, I grew stronger. That was just a basic-level, at-home fitness routine. Can you imagine the suffering Olympic athletes go through in their efforts to become the best? They know that missing even one training session can cause them to fall short of their goals. Championship-caliber athletes are focused and driven, many times to the point of becoming obsessed with the goal they are trying to achieve. Even when their muscles are screaming, they keep going. They know that the results are worth the temporary pain.

If athletes can be that dedicated when it comes to worldly objectives, should we be any less passionate about our heavenly calling? In his letter to the church in Corinth, the Apostle Paul wrote, "Do you not know that in a race all the runners run, but only one receives the prize? So run that you may obtain it. Every athlete exercises self-control in all things. They do it to receive a perishable wreath, but we an imperishable. So I do not run aimlessly; I do not box as one beating the air. But I discipline my body and keep it under control, lest after preaching to others I myself should be disqualified" (1 Corinthians 9:24–27).

For many, the idea of pushing outside of their comfort zones and living with abandon to do God's will sounds too hard. But should we be zealous about exercising our faith and passionate about living for God, even if it means suffering? Yes! Suffering is never fun, but like athletic training, it leads us to something better.

Many people in the Bible suffered. Those who ultimately submitted to God grew through the experience and became stronger in ways that God could use. Peter started out as an impetuous, opinionated fisherman. Jesus saw past his unbridled nature and said he would become a steadfast leader, a "rock." This did not happen overnight. It took pressing situations to bring out the Peter who was not afraid to share his beliefs about Jesus. When Peter denied his relationship with Jesus three times before the crucifixion, he wept over his denial and must have felt incredible shame. Yet after the resurrection, Jesus gently restored him. Peter went on to spread the gospel and to suffer persecution and eventually death for proclaiming Christ. He is an example of the power of receiving God's forgiveness and allowing God to use both our sinful natures and our trials for His glory.

Suffering often brings us to the point where we are willing, or even desperate, for something to change, especially if we are resisting God's direction in our lives. That desperation can generate positive change if it is channeled in the right way—seeking God and submitting to His will.

God's perspective is much different from our own. If He calls us to suffer, we can willingly submit to His call because we know that God sees the purpose in it. We know that God also sees its outcome far ahead of time. From our limited human perspectives, all we can see is the problem, but God knows the ultimate good He intends to bring from it.

Don't Hamper God's Plan

Have you ever tried to intervene in someone else's trial only to find that your efforts didn't seem effectual? Maybe you know someone who has a tendency to try to resolve your problems for you. Ironically, the people who care about us the most—the ones who should be encouraging us in our walks with Christ—can often be the ones who create the biggest roadblocks to God's plan. When loved ones see us suffer, instead of pointing us toward God, they often want to jump in and "fix" things, even if they don't need fixing.

For instance, if you have a college-age child who runs out of money, your immediate response might be to hand over some cash. But what if God doesn't want you to help financially? Of course God wants you to help your child, but help doesn't have to come in monetary form. What if He wants you to encourage your child to learn responsibility by getting a job, taking out a school loan, or getting involved in a work-study program? What if He wants you to stay out of the situation entirely and let Him handle it? Before you get involved, pray about it. Ask God to reveal what your actions should be.

One of my former co-workers used to regularly call me for rides, money, and other needs. My initial response was always to give her whatever she asked for. As the frequency of her calls increased, I realized that I was enabling her to be dependent on me rather than helping her do the thing she needed to do most—depend on God. Each day I got more and more frustrated by her constant calls for help. I wanted to show her the love of Christ, but I had to set up boundaries. God often calls us to give, but we should be led by Him and not simply by the circumstances before us. My error was not seeking God's guidance earlier. As a friend once told me, "When God puts people in the oven, don't turn the temperature down!"

Be Thankful. Seriously?

Perhaps you have experienced trials and felt that there was no one to help. Fortunately, even when God doesn't move in the way we want Him to, we can be assured that He is *always* there for us. He has total control and is using our trials to produce an end result that will glorify Him. Scripture says, "Rejoice always, pray without ceasing, give thanks in all circumstances; for this is the will of God in Christ Jesus for you" (1 Thessalonians 5:16–18).

Being thankful at all times goes against our natural inclinations. The world teaches us to be thankful when we get a pay raise, win a sweepstakes, or achieve something gratifying. Yet do we say "thank you" when we lose a job, discover we have cancer, or our spouse walks out of the marriage? Situations like these cut our hearts, and we can become depressed, anxious, or angry. "Thank you" is not usually the first thing that comes to mind!

Not only does God want us to be thankful in the midst of difficult circumstances, but He actually wants us to be thankful *for* them. Ephesians 5:20 says, "Giving thanks always and for everything to God the Father in the name of our Lord Jesus Christ." Thanking God for the good times is simply good manners, but thanking God for the difficult times reflects our faith and trust in Him. Showing gratitude means that we are trusting in God's sovereignty.

Of course, this is easier said than done. When trials hit, many Christians say, "God won't give you more than you can handle." This is simply not true. I believe God often gives us more than we can handle. If we could handle our trials, we wouldn't go to God or depend on Him. The Apostle Paul experienced this in his own life. In 2 Corinthians 1:8–11, he writes,

> For we do not want you to be unaware, brothers, of the afflic-tion we experienced in Asia. For we were so utterly burdened beyond our strength that we despaired of life itself. Indeed, we felt that we had received the sentence of death. But that was to make us rely not on ourselves but on God who raises the dead. He delivered us from such a deadly peril, and he will deliver us. On him we have set our hope that he will deliver us again. You also must help us by prayer, so that many will give thanks on our behalf for the blessing granted us through the prayers of many.

The wording in this passage, "so utterly burdened beyond our strength," is an eloquent description of being overwhelmed by cir-cumstances. Paul and his friends had reached the end of their strength; they faced more than they could handle. The wonderful result was that they learned to depend wholly on God. Nothing builds our faith like seeing God answer our prayers in the midst of what appear to be insurmountable obstacles.

Where do people get the idea that circumstances will never be more than they can handle? I think they get it from 1 Corinthians 10:13, which says, "No temptation has overtaken you that is not common to man. God is faithful, and he will not let you be tempted beyond your ability, but with the temptation he will also provide the way of escape, that you may be able to endure it." The word *temptation* here is talking about the temptation to sin. It isn't talking about the weight of circumstances or the problems we encounter. Essentially, this verse says that God will never put us in a situation in which we have no choice but to sin. He always provides a way out.

We can apply this verse to the temptations we face as a result of our trials too. During painful circumstances, Satan might tempt you to believe that God is no longer with you or that He doesn't care. You might be enticed to sin by not believing the Bible's promises or by disobeying God's leading. God won't leave us helpless in our brokenness. He always provides a way out through trusting and obeying Him. Part of that way out is depending on His strength instead of our own.

Many of the experiences throughout this book would be overwhelming for anyone. Some of them are the results of sin, but some of them are not. Even though we may not experience anything as dramatic as what we read in these stories, sooner or later we all face problems that we know go beyond our natural human strength. That is when we realize we have no choice but to trust God and depend on His *supernatural* strength.

However, if that's the only time we experience God, we are missing out on a truly abundant life. Jesus says, "The thief comes only to steal and kill and destroy. I came that they may have life and have it abundantly" (John 10:10). Experiencing God's power in overwhelming circumstances teaches us that we should turn to Him every moment, in good times and bad. If we fail to trust Him in easy times, we will miss the blessings He wants to give us at *all* times. We do not need God only when we are overwhelmed. He wants us to experience His peace, radiate His joy, and express His love to those around us every minute of every day. If we walk with Him, enjoy Him, know Him, and trust Him continually, we will be living the abundant life that He has for us.

Be Grateful, Not Grumpy!

At the end of 1 Thessalonians 5:18, which talks about being thankful in all circumstances, it says, "for this is the will of God in Christ Jesus for you." This verse is saying that if I do not thank God in my situation, I am outside of His will for me. That's a sobering thought! God wants us to grow to the point that we maintain our faith in His goodness no matter where we are. One person who knew that was Job. He knew that tested faith is true faith. He said, "Shall we receive good from God, and shall we not receive evil?" (Job 2:10). In the same way, do we only rejoice when God blesses us and grumble when He doesn't? That's not true faith. We should always thank Him, even when we don't feel like doing so.

If we were able to view our lives as God does, our attitudes would change. Adversity is a training ground, much like boot camp for the military, in which we are given opportunities to become stronger. When we go through pain, we can become stronger in our faith, trust God more, and grow in perseverance as we follow Jesus. Trials can help us find our hope in Christ. However, adversity is not just a training ground. It is also the battlefield, the final exam on what we have learned from God up to that point. How we respond will determine what God accomplishes through us in the lives of others.

When you become discouraged, seek comfort in prayer and in God's Word. Communicate and pray with other believers. Consider how God has carried others through difficulties, and remind yourself of how God has helped you in the past. God will reward your faithfulness. Galatians 6:9 says, "And let us not grow weary of doing good, for in due season we will reap, if we do not give up." Don't give up!

Where's Your Identity?

When you are suffering, it is important to remember your true identity. You are a beloved child of God. Scripture says, "I have been crucified with Christ. It is no longer I who live, but Christ who lives in me. And the life I now live in the flesh I live by faith in the Son of God, who loved me and gave himself for me" (Galatians 2:20). We are extremely valuable to God. This verse demonstrates how much God gave so that we could be saved. Speak this verse into your heart and meditate upon its truth. *You belong to Jesus.* He loves you and wants the best for you. Nothing in heaven or on earth can change that fact.

Sometimes we are tempted to base our value on our self-perception. Consider Christine, a woman who struggled with issues of identity. In her forties, she looked back on her life and condemned herself for all the things she felt she had done wrong. Her children weren't saved. She felt she had not done enough to pray with them or encourage them to read the Bible. She couldn't keep up with her domestic responsibilities. She was convinced that her husband could have done better than to marry her. In nearly every respect, she didn't feel that she measured up. She tortured herself with these thoughts. One day, she poured out her hurts to a childhood friend. Instead of stepping in to try to fix her problems, her friend turned Christine's attention back to her identity in Christ. Her friend directed her to Scriptures like 2 Corinthians 5:17, which reminded Christine that she is a new creation. She encouraged Christine to memorize Scriptures that spoke to her identity as a beloved, cherished child of God and encouraged her to remind herself of these Scriptures every time she was tempted to wallow in feelings of self-pity.

We should all have a low flesh-esteem, but a high Jesus-esteem. On our own we are weak and easily corrupted. Jesus said, "For apart from me you can do nothing" (John 15:5). Feeling bad about ourselves or our abilities is just realizing how weak we are and how much we need God. The good news is that the Bible says we can do all things through Him who gives us strength (Philippians 4:13).

Being a Christian is not just a *part* of your identity; it is *all* of it. It is who you are. God will equip you for whatever He has called you to do. Don't focus on yourself. Focus on the things of God. Then any self-deprecating feelings you have will begin to disappear. Paul encourages us, "Such is the confidence that we have through Christ toward God. Not that we are sufficient in ourselves to claim anything as coming from us, but our sufficiency is from God" (2 Corinthians 3:4–5). Even if you haven't accepted Jesus' free gift of eternal life, you are of immeasurable worth in God's eyes, no matter who you are or what you've done. Too many people struggle to believe they have value. We all want to matter to someone, and the truth is that we do—we matter to the Creator of the universe, the One who designed us in love.

When we are walking with God, we don't need to prove ourselves or our abilities. We don't have to make people like us or cause situations to turn out in our favor. Jesus was confident in God because "self" was never at the forefront in His life. He had clear direction and a heart to please His Father. He said, "For I have come down from heaven, not to do my own will but the will of him who sent me" (John 6:38).

You might think, *Well of course Jesus was confident. He was God.* While that is true, Jesus still faced the same trials we do. Jesus felt hunger, thirst, fatigue, and pain. He knew the grief of losing a loved one. The Bible says, "For we do not have a high priest who is unable to sympathize with our weaknesses, but one who in every respect has been tempted as we are, yet without sin" (Hebrews 4:15). He was tempted in all points, just like you and I. There is no struggle we face that Jesus did not confront. The difference is He did not sin in the midst of them.

Jesus' identity in the Father allowed Him to associate with outcasts, to be despised by the religious elite, to be rejected by those whom He loved, and ultimately lay down His life while others mocked Him. He knew that the Father held His life and that nothing ever happened to Him without the Father's permission (John 19:11). His esteem was not based on His own or others' opinions of Him; it was established by the Father.

If you struggle with insecurity, confess those feelings to God. Ask Him to replace your doubts with confidence in Him. Jesus died for you and has a plan for your life. Don't let the lies of Satan dictate who you are. Your security is in God, and your life is His.

Our ability to weather the storms of life and find true purpose and passion in the will of God starts with knowing our identity in Christ. Your true identity cannot be found in your relationships, career, home, personal appearance, or possessions. Those things are fickle and often change or deteriorate with time. In Luke 12:15, Jesus says, "Take care, and be on your guard against all covetousness, for one's life does not consist in the abundance of his possessions." If you try to find meaning, purpose, and fulfillment in anything other than God, you will be disappointed. Only God gives life.

Fear Not

Similar to focusing on self, concentrating on the difficulty of your trials will cause a wrong perspective that can bring about fear. Fear is often the result of pain that we think will never end. 1 John 4:18 says, "There is no fear in love, but perfect love casts out fear. For fear has to do with punishment, and whoever fears has not been perfected in love." Even though the process of going through trials is painful, when we emerge victorious, we develop a new response to suffering. We no longer have to fear because we realize that God is greater than anything we could ever face. We learn to trust the Lord and follow wherever He leads. God's faithfulness to us in the past helps our faith in the present. Thankfulness for the work God has done in us becomes a natural response.

What is holding you back from being all God wants you to be? He has already equipped you with all that you need so that even in suffering, you can experience joy, victory, and purpose. The Bible is one of the best weapons for growing stronger through adversity. God's Word tells us, "All Scripture is breathed out by God and profitable for teaching, for reproof, for correction, and for training in righteousness, that the man of God may be complete, equipped for every good work" (2 Timothy 3:16–17).

If we could grasp what it means to belong to God and be filled with His Spirit, we would never have a second of doubt or fear. We would walk in power, hope, and expectation, confident that He already knows what we need. All we have to do is ask, and He can help us see things from His perspective.

During trials, we have an incredible opportunity to take God at His Word. He will come through for us. There is no need to complain or feel insecure or terrified. God is in our corner, cheering us on. There are things in this world that can be scary if we allow them to bother us. Fear puts the brakes on our lives. When we are frightened, we would rather hide than venture out. By avoiding risks, however, we are hiding God's light. This is the opposite of what we are called to do. The words *fear not* appear many times in Scripture. Do you think God is trying to tell us something? We can trust Him to take care of us. He already knows how our stories end, and they are good endings.

Mike's Story

Mike's incredible testimony goes against the grain in our "anything goes" American culture. These days, believing something to be in opposition to God's moral compass identifies one as intolerant. Despite his adherence to the gay lifestyle, Mike knew in his heart that what he was doing was wrong and vowed to change. His story clearly demonstrates that nothing is too hard for God. He can take a life that is hurting and out of control and completely turn it around if we just let Him. When we offer God everything in our lives, He will use it for our spiritual growth and for His glory.

∽

I was born into a committed Christian home, and my dad and mom continue to have a strong marriage. My father was a loving spiritual leader of our family. My parents were active in the lives of my brother and me. I experienced no sexual, emotional, or physical abuse. While I know now that my family had its issues, there were none of the red flags often associated with homosexuality.

Despite this, early in my middle-class family existence I developed an attraction for men. I was sensitive, insecure, and artistic, and the other boys made fun of me. I was called a "fag" for the first time in sixth grade at my Christian school. I didn't know what it meant, but the seed of a new identity was planted.

In junior high, my intense desire to be like other boys turned into a sexual passion for them. I was mortified by my desires and vowed never to act on them or tell anyone about them. I suppressed my homosexual attraction by seeking perfection in academics and leadership, areas that seemed to be within my control. I was a top achiever throughout high school, college, and law school.

Suppressing my desires, however, did nothing to stop them. They only grew stronger. I became more religious, but my relationship with the Lord became more contrived.

Following law school, I began dating a fellow Baylor graduate named Stephanie. We had a good group of friends and were active leaders in Bible Study Fellowship. On the surface, our relationship was founded in the Lord, but it was also rooted in deception. My secret struggles continued to grow, and depression started to take hold. I pursued marriage with the hope that it would squelch rumors about my sexuality. Even more, I hoped it would "fix" me.

Stephanie and I married in September of 1994. We lived in Midland, Texas, where I was an attorney and Stephanie was a teacher. We were actively involved in church and Bible study and lived a "perfect couple" existence. All the while, my secret homosexual longings continued to fester.

In December of 1995, I discovered America Online. I was lured by AOL's chat rooms and the gay-identified people who seemed to be a lot like me. I "met" people who claimed to be Christians but who didn't seem to have a problem with homosexuality. I slowly began to withdraw from my marriage and other relationships. Finally, I told Stephanie I wanted a divorce, but I never told her why.

I later recanted my desire for a divorce and decided that I needed a career change instead. I quit my job and we moved to Lubbock, where I pursued a degree in architecture at Texas Tech University.

Sadly, my will to avoid AOL lasted about two weeks. I joined an online support group of gay men who encouraged me to accept my homosexuality. My gay-influenced research into Christian theology convinced me that this lifestyle was okay with God.

On November 1, 1996, I left Stephanie a letter on the door telling her I was gay and that I wanted a divorce. After moving out, I jumped headfirst into the gay lifestyle. I was out and proud. I attended a gay church and was determined to be a different kind of gay man—moral, upright, and non-promiscuous. I failed miserably from day one.

I expected immediate rejection from Stephanie and my family, but it didn't happen. While no one accepted what I was doing as right, they didn't reject me or cut me off. Stephanie refused to agree to a divorce. She said, "God put us together. I don't know how, but He can repair this situation."

The spiritual foundation I received in my youth held firm. As determined as I was to forge a new life, I had no peace in it. Even so, I could not fathom how my sexual orientation could be any different. So I continued to pursue my homosexual dream with gusto.

In 1997 I went to my parents' house for Easter. It was a tense weekend, and I vowed that I would file divorce papers the following week and never return there again. As I was leaving, my father gave me a book, *You Don't Have to Be Gay*. I viewed it as right-wing propaganda and took it only to appease him. However, I believe that the Holy Spirit physically caused my hands to open that book, and within two days I had finished reading it.

It was the first testimony I had ever heard of someone who had left the gay lifestyle. As the author referenced Scripture, I saw the truth. God did love me just as I was, but He could not leave me there. I sat on the floor of my sparsely furnished garage apartment and knew I had to go home to Stephanie. I argued for days with God and heard only one response to my arguments: "I love you."

Stephanie was shocked when I showed up at her door, but she accepted me home. We moved back to Midland, where my old law firm offered me my job back. We both began the arduous process of personal and emotional healing. About two months later we attended our first Exodus Freedom Conference and we realized we were not alone. We were filled with hope that God could indeed restore us as individuals and heal our marriage. There was no ministry for people struggling with same-sex attraction in Midland. A wonderful Bible study leader and Christian counselor regularly met with me and simply pointed me to Christ. He helped me unpack my true identity as a man and a child of God. During this difficult time, God brought about amazing healing and transformation in both Stephanie and me. He changed our lives.

Our former church became a huge part of our healing. Soon after my return, God prompted us to stop looking for a place to have our needs met and instead find a place to serve. We became part of a church plant called Stonegate Fellowship, and it was there that God called us into ministry. We started ministry for people impacted by unwanted same-sex attraction and shared our testimony publicly for the first time. As I shared from a stage the thing that I was most afraid of revealing, God showed us the beauty of being real. Our church responded with an amazing display of love, acceptance, and support. Stonegate ultimately hired me, a lawyer and former homosexual, to be its senior associate pastor. This church lived out the belief that Jesus Christ can change a life.

I have never figured out why I struggled with homosexuality. But I know from God's Word that He allows struggles into our lives so His power might be displayed in us and so He will receive praise. I can think of no better purpose for life than to serve as a vessel for God's glory and power. It is not about coming to grips with who I am. It is about coming to grips with who He is. That is a life worth living.

I would not trade the difficulties I went through for anything, nor would Stephanie. Our marriage is far better than it was before. God has blessed us with three wonderful children. He has grown in Stephanie and me a pure and beautiful love for each other and for Him. We know we have not fully arrived, but we also know that the end of the journey will be beyond our imagination.

Mike felt that his desires and his marriage were beyond help, but God exceeded his expectations and brought healing. If you are feeling overwhelmed by a challenge in your life, remember that you are not alone and that God can handle anything. The Apostle Paul wrote,

For I do not understand my own actions. For I do not do what I want, but I do the very thing I hate. Now if I do what I do not want, I agree with the law, that it is good. So now it is no longer I who do it, but sin that dwells within me. For I know that nothing good dwells in me, that is, in my flesh. For I have the desire to do what is right, but not the ability to carry it out. For I do not do the good I want, but the evil I do not want is what I keep on doing. Now if I do what I do not want, it is no longer I who do it, but sin that dwells within me. (Romans 7:15–20)

We may become discouraged by our desires and sinful nature. However, greater is He who is in you than he who is in the world (1 John 4:4).

God gives us His strength to live a holy life. He never asks us to do anything in our power alone. We can rely on His grace to live a life that glorifies Him, a life that is ultimately the most fulfilling. No matter what trials we encounter, whether from within or without, God will walk with us and give us strength to be victorious through them.

Want Hope?
Stop, Drop, and Roll

*A*s Karen packed for a business trip, her husband's tirade exacerbated the guilt she already felt.

"I can't believe you're leaving again," he said. "I don't want to be stuck alone with the kids for another whole week."

"It's not my fault you don't have a job," she lashed out. "Since I'm the only one bringing in money for this family, I don't have any choice but to go."

Her husband glared at her, then stormed out of the bedroom, slamming the door behind him.

Karen yanked the zipper on her suitcase and collapsed onto the bed. She wished things were different. To be honest, she didn't really enjoy traveling. She hated missing so many things her family did while she was gone. But what choice did she have?

After some quick goodbyes, she raced to the airport, barely getting on the plane before final boarding. During the layover, her final flight was cancelled, leaving her stuck in the airport another five hours waiting for the next one.

Needing to call the colleague who had agreed to pick her up at her destination, Karen reached for the phone in her purse, which she'd strapped onto her carry-on bag. It wasn't there.

Frantic, she glanced all around her. No purse. She searched every inch of the terminal she'd covered since she arrived. Karen distinctly remembered having it when she got off the first plane. Someone must have snatched it while she wasn't looking.

After finding a security guard, she explained her predicament, her words barely coming out past the lump in her throat. He didn't offer much hope.

Fighting tears, Karen collapsed into a chair at a deserted gate. She had no cell phone, no money, no credit cards, and no boarding pass. Everything in her life felt horribly out of control. She felt trapped and alone.

Can you relate to Karen's struggles? Your challenges will be different, but at their core, they may be very much the same: an overly busy life, a tendency toward self-reliance, and difficulty seeing things from the perspective of others.

Desperation Breeds Change

When we're in the middle of a crisis and life seems hopeless, many of us become desperate. Having exhausted our resources, there seems to be no solution in sight. Too often, it is only then that we turn to God. Sometimes He allows such distress because it takes us to the end of our own strength. Only then do we allow God to come in and fix our problems His way.

If your shirt suddenly caught fire, your immediate response would probably be to move quickly. Instinct tells us to run as fast as possible to escape danger. But that would only fuel the fire. Experts say to "stop, drop, and roll." The first thing you should do is *stop* moving. Next, *drop* to the ground. Then, *roll* over and over to deprive the fire of oxygen and put it out.

The same principles apply when we face a frightening situation. When we experience trials, we may feel like running away from them. But God wants us to stop what we're doing, drop the burden, and roll the situation over to Him. When we release our burden and give it to God, He can keep our troubles from scarring our spirits and hardening our hearts.

Depending completely on God when we're feeling hopeless is hard to do. That's one reason so many give up, lose hope, and turn away from Him in bitterness. God's desire, however, is for us to rely on Him during difficult times so He can bring us comfort and minister to our needs. Trials normally take us beyond our own resources. How often have you said or heard, "All I can do is pray!" When we're at the bottom, forced to rely solely on God, that's when we experience growth in our faith.

If we cling to bitterness because of a hopeless situation, we will remain locked in despair. Releasing bitterness, whether against God or someone else, frees us to receive the Lord's intervention on our behalf. No matter how much we pray for God to act, we can't experience healing if we are holding on to the anchor of bitterness. It will only weigh us down and prevent us from accessing the real resolution to our problems.

Stop and Drop

Psalm 34:19 says, "Many are the afflictions of the righteous, but the LORD delivers him out of them all." God promises to deliver those who are discouraged and battered by life and renew them with strength and courage to stand even during the toughest of times.

We can tap into that strength. If we are drowning in hopelessness, the first step is to stop following the patterns of behavior we have adopted, let go of bitterness, and forgive those who have hurt us. In Ezekiel 36:26, God makes a wonderful promise: "And I will give you a new heart, and a new spirit I will put within you. And I will remove the heart of stone from your flesh and give you a heart of flesh." A heart of stone is difficult to penetrate. Humble yourself and allow God to give you a heart that yields to Him.

If our goal is to become who God wants us to be, then we should first strive to better understand His character and find His purpose in the midst of the storm—before we attempt to solve a problem on our own.

In Psalm 13, the Psalmist expresses frustration with his situation. "How long, O LORD? Will you forget me forever?" He struggles with depression and feelings of defeat. Ultimately, the writer turns to the only true source of hope. "But I have trusted in your steadfast love," he writes. "My heart shall rejoice in your salvation. I will sing to the LORD, because he has dealt bountifully with me."

When we feel forgotten by God, we can remind ourselves of the truth of His constant presence with us. Knowing we are traveling the right road with God will keep us from drowning in our problems, even when they last longer than we expect.

Trials have a tendency to stir up emotions like fear, despair, and anger. When we release the emotional clutch we often have on our issues, we will find relief. Isaiah 26:3–4 promises, "You keep him in perfect peace whose mind is stayed on you, because he trusts in you. Trust in the LORD forever, for the LORD GOD is an everlasting rock." When we feel uncertain about our present or our future, we can depend on the certainty of God's heart and ways. Trusting in Him leads to rest.

In stark contrast, those who refuse to humble their hearts can end up in a chronic state of despair. Much effort and wealth are spent as people attempt to self-medicate through alcohol, drugs, shopping, vacations, pleasures, and other vain attempts to cover up or numb the pain of their lost hope. Many would rather do anything in their own power than hand over the reins to God. They think they are free, but in reality, they have locked themselves in bondage. By rejecting God and refusing to trust that His ways are best, they have prevented themselves from accessing the only true solution.

I am still learning about God's faithfulness in every circumstance of life myself. On one occasion, I forgot to record a check in my register. As a result, I spent more money than what was available in my account and the bank charged me an overdraft fee. I started thinking thoughts like, *No money for the next ten days, no going out to eat, no gas in the car, no groceries.* I needed $100 to cover the overdraft, and I even thought about calling my mother and asking her for a loan. I also worried about getting food and other necessities. Then I stopped and thought about all the ways God had provided for me in the past. I reflected on Philippians 4:19, which says, "And my God will supply every need of yours according to his riches in glory in Christ Jesus."

It's important to remember that our needs are much different from our wants. By stopping and remembering God's provision and reflecting on His promises, I started to drop the burden of worry and roll it over to God. I told God that I trust Him as my Provider, regardless of my circumstances. I then began to experience His peace instead of worry. I continued to think about my situation, but I chose to trust. God's answer came quickly. To my utter amazement, the same day I realized my accounting error, I received a check in the mail. It was for exactly $100. I was blown away. God is always faithful!

Are You Willing to Ask?

Perhaps you believe God helps other people, but not you. "If He hasn't helped by now," you might say, "why should I think He'll help me in the future?" It's a natural question. However, God has already helped you many times throughout your life, whether you know it or not.

God already knows our needs, but He wants us to ask Him for help. Jesus said, "Ask, and it will be given to you; seek, and you will find; knock, and it will be opened to you" (Matthew 7:7). God wants to help us through our problems. He also wants us to come to Him, humble ourselves, and ask Him to work. God wants us to acknowledge that He is our source of help so that when help comes, we know whom to thank for it.

In Matthew 9:27–29, we read about two blind men who came to Jesus to be healed. Because of their blindness, they were probably beggars and struggling to survive. When they heard that Jesus was able to do miracles, they went to Him filled with hope that He could restore their sight. Jesus asked if they believed. When they said yes, He touched their eyes and restored their sight. Jesus was ready and able to help, but these men had to ask first.

That principle has proven true in my life. Whenever I ask God to help me, He is always there, ready and willing. Sometimes I don't feel like asking God for help because I'm mad about my situation or I'm feeling sorry for myself. There have been many times when I have endured a lot of suffering before I finally asked God to step in.

In Luke 13:34, we see Jesus weeping and wailing in grief. "O Jerusalem, Jerusalem, the city that kills the prophets and stones those who are sent to it! How often would I have gathered your children together as a hen gathers her brood under her wings, and you were not willing!" Jesus was grieving over the lost state of His beloved and chosen people. He left His heavenly home and came to earth so all people, not just Israel, could be reconciled to God. Yet the Jews turned their backs on Him. It breaks God's heart when we refuse His tender ministrations.

When a child rebels against loving parents, sometimes those parents can do nothing but stand back and weep. All they want to do is bless and embrace their beloved child, but that child won't let them.

In Luke 15:11–32, Jesus tells a parable of a man with two sons. The younger son wanted his inheritance while his father was still alive. Asking such a thing was like telling his father that he wished he were dead. With great sadness, the father granted the boy's wish and gave him the money, then watched him leave. The son foolishly squandered all that had been given to him and ended up with nothing. He realized his only chance for survival was to go back to his father. Believing that he no longer deserved the position of son, he asked to be one of the servants. In verse 20, we read the father's reaction: "And he arose and came to his father. But while he was still a long way off, his father saw him and felt compassion, and ran and embraced him and kissed him." That's how God responds when we are broken and ready to return to Him.

Eddie's Story

In this testimony, we will look at the life of a man who almost lost his marriage, and temporarily lost his joy, because of his addiction to pornography. His life is proof that God can redeem even the most broken life. But it's not through our own effort that deliverance comes. It's through a willingness to surrender to God.

Around the age of ten, a childhood friend of mine found several boxes of pornographic magazines in his brother's bedroom. At the time, I thought it was a great discovery. I had no idea that I was laying the foundation on which my adult life would be built.

When I accepted Christ at the age of thirteen, I decided to put pornography out of my life. I quickly found that it had a strong hold over me. The craving for porn had become my master. When the desire called, I had to answer. It was like a drug, and the only thing I could think about was getting my fix. I could never break away for more than a few weeks at a time. One time, I even put down the Bible to obey my desires!

I would binge on porn for days or weeks at a time until I was sick of it. When I faced the real world again, I felt ashamed. I desperately wanted to be free, but I did not believe I was worthy of God's grace.

When I got married, I thought things would change, but marriage only compounded the problem. Not only did I still have the same overwhelming desires, but I now had to live a double life.

I continually sought opportunities to be home alone or to stay up late to secretly gratify this desire. My wife knew something was wrong, but she didn't know what. My deceit bred a lot of anxiety, and our marriage became full of tension.

I spent money that I could not account for. To cover it up, I became a chronic liar. I lied so regularly that it began to affect every other area of my life.

One day I took a walk in a park to pray. I spent several hours there, asking God why I couldn't gain control over this addiction. I left the park feeling that I had accomplished nothing. I had grown so distant from God that He felt a million miles away.

The next day, I returned. I again spent several hours trying to pray, but the result was the same.

I went back the next day. For the first time in my life, I felt truly broken. I realized my need for change and my inability to make it happen. I needed to surrender.

As I prayed this time, it was as if heaven opened up and God poured His power into every fiber of my being. My old desires fell away like unlocked chains. I had been set free! God's Spirit flowed through and transformed me.

Though I hadn't opened the Bible for years, many Scripture passages came to mind that I didn't remember seeing before.

When I got home, I found a Bible and a concordance. I did word searches to see if I could find the passages that had come to mind. To my amazement, I found them, some almost verbatim.

One Scripture that had a great impact on me was Romans 4:5: "And to the one who does not work but believes in him who justifies the ungodly, his faith is counted as righteousness." Another was Isaiah 61:10: "I will greatly rejoice in the LORD; my soul shall exult in my God, for he has clothed me with the garments of salvation; he has covered me with the robe of righteousness."

God freely offered forgiveness when I trusted in Jesus, who had died to pay for my sins and make me new. Once I surrendered to Him, He covered me with His salvation and wrapped His righteousness around me like a robe. I was free from my debt to God. I was cleansed, not by my own efforts, but by the grace of God. I have no righteousness of my own, but because I claim God's righteousness, I can walk with Him fully justified. I know that God loves and accepts me.

I sensed God calling me to tell my wife what I had been dealing with and confess what I had been doing. I wrote out my story and shared it with her. Our relationship was not healed overnight. It took a great deal of time, but my marriage is now better than I ever imagined possible. The irony is that it is more satisfying than any fantasy could be.

Sex was created by God to be enjoyed within the bounds of the marriage relationship, meeting the need for intimacy. Pornography is a pollution of the sexual union because it lacks personal intimacy. Porn is like a rotten apple. It appears sweet and shiny on the outside, but inside it is only decay and rot.

True intimacy satisfies the emotional, spiritual, intellectual, and physical needs of both husband and wife. Pornography robs a marriage of those things and saps the life out of the relationship. Porn is a disease of the soul that causes blindness to the reality of true intimacy.

Anything that takes the place of the good things God has designed for us will fail to satisfy. We can gratify our needs, but we cannot satisfy them. No one can be fulfilled outside of God's will.

Worldly things will always leave you empty. When you get to the point that you are weary of chasing pleasure, you will either seek God or end up in despair. If you die to yourself and surrender to Him, you will no longer be driven by your desires. Instead, you will be set free and led by the Spirit of God.

Eddie's addiction to pornography was crippling. Rather than seeking righteousness, he allowed his life to be ruled by deception and secrecy, but he never fooled God. The Father knew exactly what His child was doing behind closed doors. When Eddie finally grew tired of his empty life, confessed his sin, and surrendered, he was delivered by the grace of God. When he realized that there was no other hope, he let God do the impossible. God worked a miracle: Eddie found true marital intimacy with his wife, his self-respect was restored, and he developed a relationship with Christ that became the single most important thing in his life.

James 4:7 says, "Submit yourselves therefore to God. Resist the devil, and he will flee from you." Whether you have experienced trials of your own making or have allowed circumstantial troubles to callous your heart, God can perform a miracle inside of you. Just as He helped Eddie, God will lead you through the steps of obedience necessary for healing. Ask Him to be Lord of every area of your life and trust Him to guide you perfectly.

12

Enduring with Patience

A young Christian man went to his pastor and said, "Pastor, will you please pray for me? I have really been impatient lately, and I need more patience."

"Sure," he said. "I'll be glad to pray for you."

The young man thanked him and left.

The next day, the transmission went out in his car. Two days later, his five-year-old son fell off the swing set and had to get stitches. A few days after that, his boss informed him that he would need to put in at least sixty hours the following week to finish a major project.

Finally, the young man called his pastor. "I have been struggling more this week than before I came to see you."

"Good," the pastor replied. "My prayers are being answered."

"What do you mean?"

"I have been asking God to send you tribulation in the morning, in the afternoon, and in the evening."

"Why would you do that?" the young man asked. "I didn't ask you to pray for tribulation. I asked you to pray for patience."

"Yes," the pastor said. "But it's through adversity that we learn patience."

Godly Character Is Formed

Godly character isn't handed to us in a gift-wrapped box. It is developed through tribulation. If we pray for patience, the right perspective, or strength, God may allow trials into our lives to help us learn to endure.

From God's perspective, the whole point of suffering is to help us mature spiritually. As Paul writes, "Not only that, but we rejoice in our sufferings, knowing that suffering produces endurance, and endurance produces character, and character produces hope, and hope does not put us to shame, because God's love has been poured into our hearts through the Holy Spirit who has been given to us" (Romans 5:3–5).

Patience is a virtue we will need throughout our lives, especially when we must endure hardship. In his letter to the Galatians, Paul reminds us, "But the fruit of the Spirit is love, joy, peace, patience, kindness, goodness, faithfulness, gentleness, self-control; against such things there is no law" (Galatians 5:22–23). Patience is a fruit of the Spirit that is given to us as believers in Christ. But it doesn't come naturally. It needs to be developed.

How can we practice patience when our human tendency is to be impatient? It requires a change of attitude based on trusting God rather than our feelings, circumstances, others, or ourselves. If you lose your job, for instance, you might start the process of finding a new job by sending out résumés. When months pass and you don't receive a call, you may be tempted to think that nothing is happening and that your efforts are pointless. Instead, consider that God may be allowing you to endure an uncomfortable season of unemployment, knowing that He is faithful, trusting that He will take care of you, and believing that He is working on your behalf.

Our faith develops as we believe that something *is* happening— that God is always at work and does have a plan, even if we cannot see it. Just because we don't observe change occurring doesn't make it any less real. For instance, I don't witness grass physically growing in my backyard, but after a few weeks without mowing my lawn, my grass shows that it has been very busy indeed. We need to keep our hearts and minds focused on God during stormy seasons and try not to "watch the grass grow." When we are eager for something to come about, we often feel anxious and desire to see immediate results. Sometimes it may seem as if God isn't working because things aren't happening in the way we desire, but what is really happening is that our attitude of entitlement blurs our vision of what's really happening. When it seems like God isn't actively working in your life, He may simply be teaching you how to be patient and center your thoughts and mind on Him.

We live in an instant-gratification society. We want what we want, and we want it *now*! God does not want us to behave like spoiled children. He wants us to learn patience and be intentional about exercising this virtue.

Think about what causes you to become impatient. Perhaps you think you have so much to do that you can't waste one moment. God doesn't want our lives to be so jam-packed that we can hardly breathe. That's not an *abundant* life. It is a *bundled* life. If you are constantly busy, you will be closed to anything that happens outside of your set schedule. If God calls you to do something, will you be able to find time to do it? Will you even hear the call?

You may think you need something to happen immediately, but what if it doesn't? Will your life really fall apart? Probably not. We *want* things to happen right away, but we don't usually *need* them to. Sometimes what we really need (even though we may not feel like it at the time) is for our desires *not* to be met immediately. God knows that this way, we will have to develop new strategies for waiting.

Patience isn't a feeling. It's a choice. We can develop it by practicing patience in the little things around us. Start with people you come in contact with each day, like the drivers around you on the road or annoying bosses or coworkers at the office. Make a commitment to be patient with them, no matter what. Decide not to speak too soon, act in anger, or judge.

You may be surprised how well you do once you've committed to doing it. If you slip now and then, don't give up trying. Developing patience is well worth your time and effort.

God's Patience

The Bible provides many examples of God's unending patience. In Exodus 3–4, for example, Moses wanted to walk away from God's call to lead the Israelites out of Egypt. Even though God had prepared him for the task, Moses asked God to send someone else.

Moses listed many reasons why he wasn't the right man for the job: he wasn't important enough, he wasn't sure what to call God if someone asked His name, he was afraid the Israelites wouldn't believe him, he was not an eloquent speaker. Clearly he was more concerned about the reaction of others than following God's instructions.

Exodus 4:14 tells us that the Lord's anger burned against Moses. Yet God didn't send a lightning bolt to strike him. God simply said, "Is there not Aaron, your brother, the Levite?" Moses liked that idea. So God allowed Aaron to speak for Moses.

If God asks you to do something, can you imagine telling Him no? Yet we do it all the time. How many times have we been moved by the Holy Spirit to do something, then not followed through? Perhaps God put someone on your mind to call, but you never did. Maybe He impressed upon your heart to donate to a charity, but you didn't mail the check. Isn't that telling Him no? Fortunately, God offers second chances. We can be thankful that His patience is far more abundant than our own.

Despite Moses' hesitancy, God did miraculous things through him. Moses' wooden staff turned into a snake. When Pharaoh's magicians turned their staffs into snakes as well, Moses' snake ate theirs. Moses warned Pharaoh that plagues were coming, but the ruler didn't listen. When the plagues came, Pharaoh pleaded that they be taken away. When the Israelites were being chased by Pharaoh's army, God used Moses to make a path for the people through the Red Sea. After the Israelites had crossed to safety on dry ground, God used Moses to make the waters come together again and drown Pharaoh's army.

As the Israelites traveled in the desert, God continued to work through Moses to provide them with food, direction, and safety. Even their clothes did not wear out. Instead of being thankful for their provision, the Israelites complained against Moses and against God. As a result, God did not allow them to enter the Promised Land. They continued wandering in the hot desert until the disbelieving generation had passed away.

There were times when Moses grew impatient in leading the Israelites. He became angry when they worshipped another god (Exodus 32:19–20). He broke the stone tablets given to them by God. He called the Israelites "rebels" and struck a rock in anger (Numbers 20:10–12). Yet Moses' patience grew through his journey.

God wanted to destroy the Israelites several times for their disobedience (Exodus 32:9–11; 33:3–6), but Moses prayed that He would not obliterate the Israelites, and they were spared.

The children of Israel repeatedly refused to learn from their mistakes. God designed Canaan, a land of milk and honey, just for them. The Promised Land was beautiful. Huge grapes ripened in giant clusters, green grass swayed in the breeze, and the sea was clear and blue. But because giants lived in Canaan, the Israelites were fearful and refused to believe that God would empower them to take the land. In reality, it wasn't the giants that kept the Israelites out of the Promised Land. It was their own fear. The Israelites saw themselves as grasshoppers next to the giants. They let the enemy define them instead of listening to the promises of

God. As a consequence, that generation circled Mount Sinai for forty years on a trip that should have taken no more than two weeks. Once that generation was dead, their children were allowed to enter the land.

Problems are part of God's master plan to help us mature and become the people He wants us to be. Resisting that growth only means we will have to learn the same lessons over and over. You don't want to continue to experience the same trial for the next forty years, do you? I sure don't!

Before being called by God to lead the Israelites out of Egypt, Moses was a prince living in the palace of the Pharaoh. He was probably living a comfortable, routine life. He didn't ask for this long faith-strengthening assignment, but God disrupted that comfortable life because He had a special purpose for Moses. So it is with us. When things go well, we tend to lose some of our desire to seek God's face. It is not that we intentionally distance ourselves from Him, but when everything seems under control, we don't feel a need for God to step in. We don't realize His larger purpose until we join in His work. We don't know how dependent we are on Him until we're in difficult situations.

It is not God's plan for us to remain self-sufficient. He wants to stretch us and help us grow so we will better conform to the image of His Son. He wants to use us in His work to reach others. The world is in bad shape. Many are lost, not knowing the saving grace of Jesus Christ. God can use us to show His power to others by allowing them to see us experience peace in the midst of suffering.

Peace Doesn't Mean Painless

God's peace does not mean we won't have pain. It means that in the midst of our pain, we trust Him and experience His presence, His faithfulness, and His love. How can we patiently endure our problems? Here are some ideas.

1. Focus on the fact that God has nothing but good in store for you, whether what you experience looks good to you or not.

God acted for our good even in the beginning. Genesis 1–2 tells us that God created us in His image, blessed us, and gave us the resources of the earth and the companionship of Himself and one another. He also died for us. Romans 8:32 says, "He who did not spare his own Son but gave him up for us all, how will he not also with him graciously give us all things?" God always wants what is best for us for the purposes of His kingdom.

2. Recognize that you deserve nothing but hell (Psalm 103:10; Romans 3:23; 6:23).

This may sound harsh, but it's true. God has given us everything not because we deserve it, but out of His great love for us. Because we cannot keep from sinning, God gives us the free gift of eternal life through Jesus Christ. The Blameless One took our sin upon Himself. When Jesus died on the cross, He descended into hell, the place we deserve to go. He is now the Mediator, and He has won the victory over sin. Everything we experience is filtered by God's grace.

3. Believe that God uses everything for your betterment.

In times of trouble, many people like to quote Romans 8:28: "And we know that for those who love God all things work together for good, for those who are called according to his purpose." Ironically, the next verse is often overlooked: "For those whom he foreknew he also predestined to be conformed to the image of his Son, in order that he might be the firstborn among many brothers" (v. 29). The way God causes things to work together for good is through our transformation. He uses all things, including suffering, to give us the same perspective and endurance as Christ. Ultimately, His purpose is for us to become more like Jesus. That's the most loving thing He can do.

God is preparing us to be heavenly creatures, but He has good plans for us on earth too. In Mark 10:29–30, Jesus says, "Truly, I say to you, there is no one who has left house or brothers or sisters or mother or father or children or lands, for my sake and for the gospel, who will not receive a hundredfold now in this time, houses and brothers and sisters and mothers and children and lands, with persecutions, and in the age to come eternal life."

The good things God has planned for us are not reserved only for heaven. He also wants our lives here to be full and abundant.

My Cancer Story

In the midst of writing this book, God allowed a trial to come into my life that tested my trust and patience in a way I had never experienced before. I hope my testimony will encourage you in whatever trials you may face.

෴

I experienced stomach and abdominal pain for several years. I finally had a colonoscopy to find out what the problem was. A week later, my doctor called and asked me to come to his office. When I arrived, he said, "Emily, I found something that appeared abnormal in your small intestine. I took a biopsy and sent it to the Mayo Clinic. The report says you have cancer."

That's impossible, I thought. *Nobody in my family has cancer!* My emotions churned and my stomach was tied in knots. Then I thought of Philippians 4:6–7: "Do not be anxious about anything, but in everything by prayer and supplication with thanksgiving let your requests be made known to God. And the peace of God, which surpasses all understanding, will guard your hearts and your minds in Christ Jesus."

As I sat there, stunned, I asked God to fill me with His peace. A divine calm instantly took over my heart, and I was able to thank Him for allowing this trial in my life. I even started thinking of ways to minister to those around me.

That night, I talked to a friend who is a cancer survivor. He was such an inspiration that I actually felt excited about going through this experience. My situation hadn't changed, but God had changed my perspective on it.

God took me out of my day job temporarily and placed me into a new mission field. During my medical exams and consultations, I ended up in places I probably wouldn't have otherwise gone to share Jesus. But I determined that if only one life could be changed through my experience, it would be worth the cost.

The only thing I had to offer was my availability, so I prayed that the people I came in contact with would see Jesus in me more than they would see the cancer. I wanted to be faithful in taking care of God's work because of God's faithfulness in taking care of me.

It was God's time to shine and my time to serve Him. I decided to be a vessel He could use to share His love in ways people might not normally experience. I told others, "I'm not dying from cancer. I'm only living with it temporarily. I had the flu before, and I got over that too."

I had been diagnosed with lymphoma, which tends to spread, so we had to quickly find out if the cancer was anywhere else in my body. The oncologist scheduled a battery of tests, at least one each day for two weeks. Thankfully, they all came back negative, indicating that the cancer was contained in just one area of my small intestine.

The next step was to meet with the stem-cell specialist who would determine my course of treatment. The possibilities included chemotherapy alone or surgical removal of the cancer combined with chemotherapy. My primary oncologist had already decided to begin chemotherapy, but the stem-cell specialist recommended I first see a surgeon and explore having the lymphoma removed. I would begin chemotherapy six to eight weeks later. I met with the surgeon and he scheduled my operation for the following week.

In my time of need, I had to let others minister to me. This was a role I rarely had to assume before. My mom read devotionals to me every day in the hospital. People came to visit, sent cards, brought meals, texted Scriptures and prayers, and did things for me that I couldn't do for myself. I had to let others take care of me and pray over me. Throughout the ordeal, I was blessed and humbled by the tremendous support of my church family and many others who were praying for me.

The tumor was successfully removed during my first surgery, but within a few days, I began vomiting and running a fever. I had to have a second surgery to treat a serious infection that had resulted from the first. Two days later, the surgeon told me he needed to go back in again to make sure the infection was gone. Upon hearing the news, I burst into tears. I couldn't imagine going through a third surgery and being in more pain than I already was. Yet I chose to trust that the doctor knew what was best.

After three surgeries, I lay on the hospital bed, in and out of a drug-induced mental fog. As the pain medications wore off, I felt excruciating pain and was desperate for more medication.

Although I trusted my doctor, ultimately it was God I trusted for complete healing. I asked Him to relieve my pain and heal my body. I prayed, "God, Your Word says in Psalm 30:2, 'O LORD my God, I cried to you for help, and you have healed me.'" I then reflected on Proverbs 3:5–6: "Trust in the LORD with all your heart, and do not lean on your own understanding. In all your ways acknowledge him, and he will make straight your paths."

In spite of my trust in God for complete recovery, I was impatient with the slower-than-anticipated healing process. I thought I would be back to living a normal life within a short time. Instead, I remained in the hospital for three more weeks.

As my impatience kicked up a notch, I recalled Romans 12:12, which says, "Rejoice in hope, be patient in tribulation, be constant in prayer." I decided to use this time for God's kingdom. I shared God's love and prayed over the nurses I met. I handed out crosses, devotional books, and plates with Scripture on them. Often, my testimony was met with surprise. Yet I was eager to tell people that God loves and cares for them so much that He died on the cross and was waiting for them to come to Him. Only God knows the lives that were impacted during that time.

Toward the end of my hospital stay, the doctor reported that the latest pathology report revealed absolutely no signs of cancer. That meant I would need no chemotherapy or radiation. The cancer was *gone*! I was overwhelmed with gratitude for God's miraculous answer to prayer. I thought my trial was finally over, so I was disappointed when the doctor told me I would have an additional week or two of recovery at home.

When I was finally released from the hospital, I expected to recover within the predicted two-week time frame. My recovery took longer. As I struggled to regain my strength, I became frustrated and anxious. Once again, I recognized that my impatience revealed a lack of trust in God and that I needed to repent. I prayed, "Lord, I recognize my impatience. Forgive me, and help me trust You completely with my life and my healing process." Then I read Psalm 119:71, and I felt as if it had been written especially for me: "It is good for me that I was afflicted, that I might learn your statutes."

The human body is gifted with the ability to create new cells to replace the older ones as they die off. Cancer occurs when this normal and necessary function is disturbed, allowing abnormal cells to grow without limits. This is also a picture of what happens when we cease to place our trust in God.

It is normal to be concerned when we face trials. When we address those concerns the right way, we reap tremendous blessings because we are following God's pattern for living. For instance, becoming concerned with our eternal destiny leads us to acknowledge our need for a Savior and to respond to His free gift of eternal life.

When we are in the middle of a trial, we can trust Him to see us through it. We don't have to face things alone and simply hope it all works out. If we fail to trust Him during those times, we are allowing for the proliferation of a cancer. Abnormal growths of worry and bitterness abound when we refuse to let trials create the peaceable fruit of righteousness by running to God with our problems. If such growths aren't removed, they will negatively affect our lives in every area. In the end, dealing with our issues God's way causes far less damage than letting them get out of hand or trying to handle them on our own.

If you're at a place where you need open heart surgery without the anesthesia (spiritual surgery), don't resist God's wise and loving intervention. He loves you beyond measure. He knows what is best for you and will work things out for your good and His glory.

Conclusion

*I*f you put your open hand into a river, the water will flow between your fingers as it moves along. Everything in your life flows through God's hands before it reaches you. When the circumstances of life hurt, don't try to stop the flow of water. You can trust the One who's controlling it.

When the waves of life bounce you around mercilessly, is your sole desire to calm the sea? Jesus' disciples felt that way. In Matthew 8:23–27, they were in a panic over a storm that was tossing them about. They were convinced they were going to die and did not understand how Jesus could sleep through it. Perhaps they thought He had hit His head on something and was knocked out. After all, who could sleep through that racket? But Jesus knew who had control—His Heavenly Father. The disciples could have experienced the same peace Jesus had, but they chose not to.

God allowed them to go through the storm because it enabled them to witness His power through Jesus. God allows us to go through storms for the same reason. Storms provide amazing opportunities to see the power of God working through us—very often in ways we would not see without them.

Some people believe that children of God should never struggle. If you're struggling, you may think you must be doing something wrong. That perspective is not biblical. Trials are part of everyday life in a fallen world. While they can be a sign that you are out of God's will and that He is trying to get your attention, that's not always the case. Sometimes trials happen even when we are obedient and doing all we can to follow Him.

God allows us to experience pain and suffering because He refuses to leave us as we are. Rather than giving us lives free from struggle, God actually promises that our lives will contain challenges and trials. He uses these things to teach us and to help us grow into spiritual maturity.

During trials, we need hope. Some people place their hope in friends or family. Others place it in a strong financial portfolio. Others place it in finding true love, or in a spouse. Hope springs from something we think will remove our pain. But true hope is not the promise of total relief from suffering. It is the knowledge that God is doing something through our suffering and that we will find something better on the other side.

Psalm 62:5 says, "For God alone, O my soul, wait in silence, for my hope is from him." Hebrews 10:23 encourages us, "Let us hold fast the confession of our hope without wavering, for he who promised is faithful."

There is a stark difference between the hope of which the Bible speaks and the hope the world offers. The world's hope is based on wishful thinking. Biblical hope is based on the unshakable, unchangeable character of God. God knows all things and is in control of all things. He is always present, and His words determine the outcome of our trials. Once God speaks something, it is done. "And God said, 'Let there be light,' and there was light" (Genesis 1:3).

Our hope is based on the knowledge that God is working things out according to our best interest. He knows the things in our hearts that need to be revealed, tested, or changed. He knows that difficult circumstances are the right tools to accomplish that goal. He knows what we truly need, and He uses our circumstances—good and bad—to accomplish what is best for us.

The testimonies in this book are examples of how God uses pain and suffering to transform the lives of His children. They also show how beautiful the results can be. These people experienced God in a special way, and you can too. Just as He was ready and able to help in their circumstances, He is ready and able to help in yours.

I pray this book has enabled you to see your trials and struggles as opportunities to renew your mind and let go of old patterns in order to live a life free of doubt and fear. I also hope that you have begun to see problems not as something to avoid at all costs, but as stepping stones to help you climb to the next level of spiritual maturity. I hope the testimonies included here have helped you realize how much God cares and that He is in control of every situation.

If you have struggled with your attitude toward the problems God has allowed you to experience, why not commit to a new attitude? When something upsetting happens, ask God for His view on things.

When you trust God in this way, He can show you solutions to life's challenges you never could have seen on your own. He always gives wisdom to those who seek Him (James 1:5).

When life hurts, get on your knees. When it hurts more, dig more deeply into the Scriptures. When the pain won't let up, increase the time you spend with fellow believers. Memorize passages from the Bible that are especially meaningful to your situation and speak them aloud. Write them down and post them on your mirror or refrigerator—whatever it takes to get God's Word into your heart.

Eventually, your relationship with God will become stronger, your perspective and priorities will change, and your spirit will be more sensitive to God's leading. The answers will become clearer as you lean on God's power rather than your own. The Psalmist says, "God is our refuge and strength, a very present help in trouble" (Psalm 46:1).

While you wait for God's answers, renew your mind daily with the living Word of God. Scripture says, "For the word of God is living and active, sharper than any two-edged sword, piercing to the division of soul and of spirit, of joints and of marrow, and discerning the thoughts and intentions of the heart" (Hebrews 4:12). Search the Scriptures, pour your heart out to God, then sit quietly and listen. Allow the Holy Spirit to minister to you. Refuse to entertain thoughts of doubt and dread. Look at your problems as opportunities for God to shine through you.

If you follow the Master Designer's plan, you will experience victory. Jesus died to set you free. He loves you so much that He took the nails in His hands and feet and suffered a cruel death on the cross. Do you know what He was thinking about the whole time? You! Embrace that truth with everything you have and never take it for granted. Don't ever forget how precious you are to Him.

Remain faithful to God because He will always be faithful to you. As James wrote, "Draw near to God, and he will draw near to you" (James 4:8). No matter the challenges you are facing, I pray that you will experience the deep and abiding faithfulness of God, whose tender mercies never fail.